Out of the Comfort Zone

Out of the Comfort Zone

Is Your God Too Nice?

R. T. Kendall

Hodder & Stoughton
LONDON SYDNEY AUCKLAND

Copyright © 2005 R. T. Kendall

First published in Great Britain in 2005

The right of R. T. Kendall to be identified as the Author of
the Work has been asserted by him in accordance
with the Copyright, Designs and Patents Act 1988.

10 9 8 7 6 5 4 3

British Library Cataloguing in Publication Data
A record for this book is available from the British Library

ISBN 0 340 86293 9

Typeset in Bembo by Avon DataSet Ltd,
Bidford-on-Avon, Warwickshire

Printed and bound in Great Britain by
Bookmarque Ltd, Croydon, Surrey

The paper and board used in this paperback are natural
recyclable products made from wood grown in sustainable forests.
The manufacturing processes conform to the environmental
regulations of the country of origin.

Hodder & Stoughton
A Division of Hodder Headline Ltd
338 Euston Road
London NW1 3BH
www.madaboutbooks.com
www.hodderbibles.co.uk

To Jack and Charles

Contents

Foreword

There are two primary methods the devil deploys to harm or destroy the Church of Christ – *Murder* and *Mixture*. In the first he seeks to intimidate and kill God's servants, and by the second, seduce them into error. The first leads to sudden and violent death. The other draws us slowly to an inexorable death 'by a thousand cuts'. Of the two, the latter is surely the most dangerous, because though the first method may cause us to lose our *lives*, the second results in the complete loss of our *testimony*. The Church thus becomes a spent force, lost for words, and completely assimilated by that very world she is meant to challenge and transform by her message. The salt has not only lost its savour, but the pepper has lost its pep!

This book therefore needed to be written. Prophets are people who hear what others cannot hear, see what others cannot see, and then dare to say what others daren't say. A sense of compulsion in the heart of the author combined with the pressing needs of the hour are two of the best reasons for writing a book, and the result here is a prophetic and very timely word.

When I was a young theological student in London during the late 1970s, for two years my wife and I regularly heard Dr R.T. Kendall preach from the historic pulpit of Westminster Chapel. I was frequently struck back then by the consistent freshness, forcefulness, and originality of his thinking, speaking and writing. R.T. was saying things no one else dared to say, and saying them with boldness, timeliness and great effect. He helped impart more of both the fear of God and the comfort of God to me. I am thrilled that he continues this vital ministry to this day.

Here, R.T. tackles some of the most destructive issues seducing even Christian leaders into compromise today. The *new* isn't always the *true*, and R.T. addresses the ferment thrown up by such matters as our lame and sub-biblical concepts of God and his sovereignty and the subsequent widespread loss of the fear of God in the Church and in the world, along with our often mixed motives for ministry. He confronts our unwillingness to cause even *necessary* offence, or to take the slightest personal risk. He calls us to abandon our pseudo-religious resistance to the work of the Holy Spirit, our lack of clarity over God's judgment and hell, and our chronic reluctance to conduct our whole lives for an audience of One. Most of us really need to hear these challenges, again and again.

He invites us, along with the author of the Epistle to the Hebrews, to shamelessly join Jesus our Master and '*go to him outside the camp, bearing the disgrace he bore*' (Heb. 13:13). Sometimes, loyalty to Christ and his message involves the experience of being stigmatised, mocked and charged with accusations of becoming 'dated' and 'irrelevant' by our critics.

But the best help we can offer to our wayward culture is not one of sycophantic conformity to it in both intellectual thinking and adulterated lifestyle, but to be out of step with those times, 'marching to the beat of a different drum'.

Unlike Samson, we dare not finish our days shorn of our power. We most accurately represent the Living God when we are truly biblical and authentically ourselves. We are most relevant when we are seemingly irrelevant. We are most likely to touch the hearts of the unfaithful when we ourselves are faithful. It is not, therefore, a case of 'out with the old and in with the new', but rather, 'out with the old and *in with the even older*'! We are to make it our aim to *get back to the Bible*.

This book is for all those who want to know how to 'rock the boat' for Jesus. R.T. attempts to show us here precisely how we can do this. In my view, he has succeeded admirably.

Greg Haslam
Minister, Westminster Chapel, London
July 2004

Preface

This is the most difficult book I have written – from several standpoints. First, I wrote this book chapter after chapter with fear and trembling, knowing it might not make me many friends and also causing me to worry if I might even lose some! I did not intend it to be controversial but I fear, upon reflection, it may be seen that way. I have never liked being controversial, much less to be seen in that manner, but sometimes I suppose you cannot help it.

Second, I have struggled to get it done. Never before have I had so much trouble with computers, for example. On more than one occasion I lost whole chapters by pushing the wrong button on my computer. After the book was completely written, with a rereading and final editing to be done, we had a storm here in the Florida Keys and the electricity went off; when it came back on, my work of several days of editing and correcting was down the drain. I don't know how it happened but it did.

Third, we wrestled over what to call this book. My original title was 'Your God is Too Nice', borrowing of course from J.B. Phillips' classic *Your God is Too Small*. But friends I trust persuaded me against it. And then, once it was completed, one of them decided that was the best title after all! But by then Hodder already had the cover designed and finished. I think my friends feared I would put the reader off by a title that was too forbidding – or that I would make people think I was presenting a God who was overly harsh and remote. Rob Parsons, for one, said, 'R.T., nobody has persuaded me more than you that "God is for me" – are you going to write a book that takes this away?' No! But I was all the more careful to preserve our teaching on the mercy and tenderness of God.

Fourth, literally days before this book went to press, we received disturbing news about Paul Cain, from whose early ministry I had drawn a number of anecdotes and quotations to help illustrate some of this book's arguments. We have had to edit certain things, leaving other things in, owing to time constraints. This news has been one of the most difficult ordeals for me personally in my whole life. I can say no more at this stage. I plead for your understanding and also for your prayers for Paul Cain.

I once promised Rob Parsons that I would never again ask him to read a manuscript, knowing how busy he is. He has helped me so much with previous books, among them *The Anointing*, *In Pursuit of His Glory* and *Thanking God*, for a start. But I went to him on bended knee again, because I knew I needed a sharp mind who would not tell me what I wanted to hear but what I needed. People like Rob, also Lyndon Bowring, are among those whose wisdom I am so blessed to have the benefit of. But there are others – Robert

Amess and Colin Dye in the UK, Dr Michael Eaton of
Nairobi, Dr Harry Kilbride, Robert Ferguson and Richard
Oates in the USA. And of course Beryl Grogan, my former
secretary, for her invaluable role in helping us put the book
together. This is to say nothing about my wife Louise who
is always faithful in telling me what I need to change – or
leave out. Our friend Nancy Wall did a good bit of research
for me in the preparation of this book. I thank God for
every bit of wisdom and loving criticism I received from
these.

It was my editor David Moloney of Hodder & Stoughton
who came up with the title of this book – *Out of the Comfort
Zone: Is Your God Too Nice?* I do feel at the end of the day this
one works best and says pretty much what I want to convey.
As always, it is a pleasure to work with David and his staff at
Hodder. I thank Trisha Dale who has done the copy-editing
and also Julie Hatherall for her input. I am grateful to God
that he has given me favour with Charles Nettleton and the
people of Hodder.

I am especially grateful that my brilliant successor Greg
Haslam, minister of Westminster Chapel, has written the
wonderful Foreword. He too has made suggestions which I
have taken on board. I knew he would agree with the thrust
of this book and I am so happy for the ongoing relationship
with him and my former friends and members of the
Chapel.

Finally, this book is dedicated to my two close friends and
colleagues Jack Taylor and Charles Carrin. When Louise and
I came to America in February 2002 I was virtually unknown
and without any ministry in the United States. They have
opened doors for me through the three of us holding Word,
Spirit and Power conferences all over America. I love these

men very much and with honour and deep affection I
dedicate this volume to them.

R.T. Kendall
Key Largo, Florida
www.rtkendallministries.com
November 2004

Introduction

The Man who was Known in Hell

'Jesus I know, and I know about Paul, but who are you?'

Acts 19:15

Nearly fifty years ago, when Paul Cain was the young 'boy wonder' – known as a faith healer and a prophet – he held nightly services in a church in the American Midwest. One night as he was preaching a lady stood and began speaking in tongues while he spoke. He stopped preaching and asked her please to stop what she was doing as it was disruptive, certainly not in the Spirit and utterly out of order. The following night as he preached she did it again – speaking in tongues as he preached. He stopped and asked again that she refrain from this but warned her this time that he would reveal what the Lord had shown him about her if she did not stop. Would you believe that on the third night she repeated the same behaviour and

1

Paul warned her to stop or he would indeed reveal what the Lord had shown him about her. She continued. He then looked at her and said that not only was she not in the Spirit but that she was living in immorality. But there was more: the man with whom she was having an affair was seated right there in the congregation – Paul pointed him out before all present – and stated that this man was planning to leave his own wife and children for her after that very service was over. The woman stopped. All was deathly quiet.

That is not the end of the story. After the service, just before the host pastor of the church took Paul to his hotel, the pastor said, 'Paul, I am closing down the meeting.'

'Why?' said Paul. 'The services are going okay.'

'Well', said the pastor, 'nobody is being converted and I feel we should discontinue having services.'

'Oh', said Paul to the pastor. 'That is not the reason you are stopping the meeting. You are closing down the meeting because I revealed what was going on between the lady and that man seated not far from her – because that very man has promised to give you a million dollars for your new church building.'

'That's a lie', the pastor countered abruptly.

'Oh', said Paul tearfully. 'I wish you had not said that. You will not live to preach in your new building.'

'Now Paul, don't say that. Please take that back.'

'I'm so sorry', Paul replied. 'I cannot take it back.'

The pastor pleaded, 'Please, Paul, don't say that. Look here, when things settle down I will have you back to preach.'

One day, several hundred miles away from that city, Paul received a phone call. It was from a member of the same church in the Midwest where Paul had been two years before. It was the day of the dedication of the new church building. The pastor had had a heart attack in the vestibule as he was walking into the auditorium and had been taken to hospital. Would Paul please pray for the pastor? But the pastor died two weeks later without returning to the church.

There is something worse, however, than the story I just related. I have to report that since I wrote the above lines – in other words, after this book you hold in your hands was finished and edited – it is now in the public domain that this same Paul Cain is a fallen hero. He has been involved in a moral failure and will no longer be in the ministry. He is now yesterday's man, like King Saul, as I wrote in my book *The Anointing: Yesterday, Today, Tomorrow.* I never dreamed in my wildest imagination this could happen to him. But God has judged this venerable prophet in an unmistakable manner. It puts in bolder relief than anything I could say in this book that God is no respecter of persons and will bend the rules for none of us. I can only think of King Saul who had such a brilliant beginning (see 1 Sam. 10:9; 11:7) and who continued to prophesy even while trying to kill David (1 Sam. 19:23f). How does one explain his gift being in operation even though the Lord had departed from him (1 Sam. 18:12)? It is because the gifts and calling of God are irrevocable (Rom. 11:29).

As I write these lines Paul Cain, aged seventy-five is somewhere in seclusion. Those who have been blessed by his ministry will be shocked. He was the last person I would have anticipated to become yesterday's man. I thought I knew him fairly well. But I have also said many times that those people I began to admire too much disappointed me sooner or later. It is equally a reminder that God will deal with you and me if we are not accountable to trusted and reliable people. Peter said that judgment must begin at the house of God (1 Pet. 4:17) – and that is certainly what has happened in the case of Paul Cain. I do not see any way he can be used again. He will now possibly be remembered more for his failure than his stunning prophecies. A nice God overlooks sin. But the God of the Bible is not nice.

Whatever is so wrong with being nice? I certainly want to be nice. But, given the way the word can be used today, I am not sure I always want to be known as nice! I have done a little research on the word, even tracing its history from the fifteenth century. Then it bore little resemblance to the way it is understood today. That is no doubt why you do not find the word 'nice' once in the Authorised Version of 1611. It is more of a modern word and is essentially a tepid word – like water that is neither cold nor hot but merely lukewarm. Using it today is sometimes (not always) a cunning way someone 'damns with faint praise' when they don't particularly admire or like the person. 'He's a nice man', they might say.

The word 'nice' today is generally used two ways – meaning either 'likeable' or that someone or something is precise. It is the first category we have in mind in this book or, to extract from various dictionaries: to be inoffensive, people-pleasing, safe, co-operative, sweet, harmless, well-mannered, friendly, hunky-dory, groovy, lovely, seemly, winsome, agreeable, delightful, ducky or yielding.

Someone helping me with my research on this book labelled one folder 'Nice God'. It made me laugh. It is the way I might approach a dog, if I was not sure if he would be friendly, 'Nice dog, nice puppy, nice dog.' And yet I think many want to feel exactly that way about God – 'Nice God, nice God.'

Really?

This book is not intended to be critical of any particular person. I cannot deny that certain people or movements enter my mind when I am discussing a particular situation that I feel needs to be addressed. I can assure you, nothing is said to let another feel they should take something personally. To be totally candid with you, I need the truth to which this book points more than anybody. I know what it is to be convicted when I preach and in fact I have been convicted as I have written this book. What follows therefore hits me right, left and centre.

And yet I wrote *Worshipping God* when I still had so much to learn about worship, *Total Forgiveness* when I was still struggling, *Pure Joy* when I knew I needed joy more than anybody I knew. So do not think I am on a pedestal looking down at you or anyone else. The truth is, I have learned over the years that often as I am preaching or writing I am on a steep learning curve myself.

I had the privilege of having Dr George Buttrick as a visiting professor of preaching when I was at Southern Baptist Theological Seminary years ago. He was an old-fashioned liberal and I got little out of his writings or even his preaching, but I never will forget one thing he hammered away at us – and I fear I have a lot yet to learn on this: 'Never moralise.' He thought preaching that is constantly moralising, telling off the audience or pointing the finger is not good preaching. I think he was almost right. Not entirely, however, because the Word of God was given to us partly for 'rebuking'

(2 Tim. 3:16). But at the same time I knew what he meant. I pray with all my heart that what you read will not make you feel 'told off'. Even if it 'hits where it hurts' I pray that you feel that the Holy Spirit is lovingly seeking to get your attention. God has been so gentle with me when getting my attention. I can never forget James 3:17: 'But the wisdom that is from above is first pure, then peaceable, gentle, and easy to be intreated, full of mercy, and good fruits, without partiality, and without hypocrisy' (AV). O Lord, let this book be full of mercy!

I want this book to bring us back to the God of the Bible. Not the God you like or the way you wish he were. But the very God of the Bible – unembellished, unvarnished – as he really is. This does not mean you will like him. I am not going to make him 'likeable' because he isn't always that. Like it or not, he simply is not a nice God. For some this book might even be an introduction to the God of the Bible. I wonder how many people know him – or even know much about him. Do you? After all, this is the only God there is. There is no other God – true God – other than the God who is portrayed, unveiled and presented than the God of the Bible – from Genesis to Revelation.

I was trained at Southern Baptist Theological Seminary before it became the theologically conservative institution it is today. When I was there over thirty years ago we had teachers and professors who would unashamedly say, 'I know Paul said that in Romans, but I disagree with Paul. I know Luke said that, but I disagree with him.'

Within the Christian Church today, speaking generally, there are those who admittedly and openly dislike the God of the

Bible. They say so. They refer to the Bible only when a verse or point of view in Holy Scripture happens to cohere with their own. But there are also those who would claim to adhere to and love the God of the Bible but interpret him in such a manner that he becomes . . . nice. Just nice. The Church today, speaking generally, has lost its way.

I fear that the God many people worship today is 'Feuerbach's God'. Ludwig Feuerbach (1804–72), the German philosopher whose writings laid the foundation for the philosophy of Karl Marx, claimed that God is nothing more than man's projection upon the backdrop of the universe. His point was this. Ordinary people need and want very much to believe there is a God or someone 'up there' who is looking after them and who will give them heaven when they die. People like this create such a God in their minds because they need this God as a crutch – to help them in their troubles. It is not that this God objectively exists – no. He exists in our imagination and, though this is subjective, we none the less objectify him, as it were, and put him 'there' so we can believe in him and worship him. That was basically what Feuerbach taught on this matter.

He had a point. I think that is sadly what many of us in the modern Church have done. We are embarrassed about the God of the Bible, especially the God of the Old Testament – and even the teachings of Jesus and the apostles when it comes to the need and the only way to be saved, God's right to judge and (last but not least) hell. So we attempt to have our cake and eat it too – to claim we believe the Bible but water down so much of what it clearly says that we become quite comfortable with 'our God', thank you very much, who – for want of a better descriptive adjective – is, simply, nice. Lovely. Sweet. Groovy. Cool. Neat.

But is that the total picture? I don't think so. I want to say some things in this book that I think need to be said. I have waited for someone else to do it. In my research I have come across an article or two, 'Your God is too nice' or 'Your God is too safe', but as far as I know there is no book addressing some of the things I feel I must bring up in this book. I want to call a spade a spade but it is the composite picture – not any group or individual – I have in mind. The truth is, we all need help in this area.

Perhaps some want God only to look nice. Some people are embarrassed that a number of our forebears, some educated, some uneducated, stressed things today that would not appeal to non-Christians. They gave Christianity, it is believed, a 'bad name', and we have inherited this. Some want to shed this image once and for all. Some theology departments and seminaries have consequently sought to turn out ministers and clergymen who will give God a 'better press'. Some are also sensitive to the criticism some non-Christians make of the Church and want to be there – right on the spot – so say, 'Hang on, that is not what I believe', as if this will cause everybody to say, 'Oh good, I will now be a Christian.' Has our apologising for the way God is perceived by many worked? Has it brought tens of thousands into our churches?

No. You know it and I know it.

I would like to think that if we stopped apologising for God – or gave up trying to make him look appealing – we would have greater success. And yet maybe not. But I know we would have his approval. I believe that if we thoughtfully hold up the

God of the Bible as he himself chose to describe himself in his Word, he will honour this. I would predict that to the degree we do that will be the degree to which the Holy Spirit will work more than ever, convert more people than ever and bring more awareness of the true God than anything that has been seen.

When I refer to 'apology' the reader should know this word is used generally two ways. One usage is 'to make an excuse for' – that is, to apologise and say one is sorry for things, etc. I fear this is the kind of apology that has prevailed in many places. There is another use of the word which is valid; that is 'to make intellectual claims for the God of the Bible that can be defended and tested by reason and facts'. This latter kind of apology is sometimes needed – as long as it is the true God that is being defended.

But the Nice God that I am uneasy with is the one people are increasingly beginning to perceive and portray in many quarters – and he is not big enough, strong enough, awesome enough or knowledgeable enough to harm a flea.

One of my predecessors at Westminster Chapel, Dr Martyn Lloyd-Jones, used to make me laugh when he would often say, 'The trouble with the Church today is that it has too many nice men in the ministry.' I think he felt that the Church needed men who were not always so pleasant but more rugged and unafraid to step on people's toes. Is he right? Do you think that many in the ministry are nice? Look around. Would you say that most of the ministers, pastors, church leaders and clergymen you know are 'nice people'? If so, was Dr Lloyd-Jones right that this is not a good thing? But I must ask, would people who know me call me a 'nice man'? I suspect that many would. And yet it does not matter what people would call you or me. I once heard Paul Cain say, 'I am too old now to disobey God.' I know exactly what he meant by that. He did not mean that he could not disobey God; we never outgrow the potential for disobedience. What he meant was that, knowing he has a limited number of days and years left to live, he cannot afford to come short of what honours the true God. That's me. I do not want to waste the time I have left to be a pleaser of people, to cater to the majority, to avoid the truth – to be a fraud.

As I said in my book *The Anointing: Yesterday, Today, Tomorrow* there are two things we all by nature want to avoid: moving outside our comfort zone and a stigma. Our Nice God keeps us safely snug in our comfort zone. We have satisfied ourselves with a belief in God and that – to so many of us – is enough. I think of James' admonition: 'You believe that there is one God. Good! Even the demons believe that – and shudder' (Jas. 2:19). But do we shudder? Are we afraid of him? Probably not. Should we be? Yes. That is why I write this book.

Once we project Nice God on the backdrop of the universe we comfort ourselves in one stroke and sometimes think that we have done our duty. Nothing else bothers us. We are in good shape. We 'do not need a thing'. And yet in that moment the One whose eyes are like a flame of fire says on his throne: 'You do not realise that you are wretched, pitiful, poor, blind, and naked' (Rev. 3:17). I would like to believe that this book will help us realise that our tepid, lukewarm devotion to the God of the Bible makes him sick and he is ready to spit us out of his mouth.

One of my fears in publishing this book is that it will play to the gallery of self-righteous Christians. There are always those who will agree with a lot in this book and will say, 'Good – give it to them.' This will not bless me and probably will not honour God. This is a book that I hope will make a definite difference in people. Good people. Nice people. Not-so-nice people. I want to stir you up, not play into any part of your comfort zone. Nice isn't good enough.

We need a fearless, rugged commitment to the God of the Bible we are prepared to die for. My friend Joseph Tson says, 'The most dangerous person in the world is a person who is not afraid to die.' We need Christians who are a threat to Satan as much as certain terrorists are to the West. I wish I were that. We are too much like the sons of Sceva who were intrigued with the supernatural underworld but no threat to Satan. Indeed, the devil didn't even know them! When trying to cast out devils in Jesus' name, claiming to know Paul and promoting themselves to the level of their incompetence, they were utterly overcome by demonic powers (Acts 19:16). They tried *using* Jesus' name but the evil spirit answered, 'Jesus I know, and I know about Paul, but who are you?' (Acts 19:15).

My old friend Rolfe Barnard used to preach a sermon entitled 'The man who was known in hell' (based on the aforementioned verse). In other words, Paul was a real threat to Satan, he was well known in the evil world. 'I want to be known in hell', said Rolfe in that unforgettable sermon. But are we? I don't mean to be unfair, but do you really think that you are a threat to the devil? Is he aware of you? Is he working overtime to keep you from threatening his interests?

Should you ask how *you* could be a threat to the devil and have a well-known reputation in hell for being a harm to the evil powers, I answer with a series of questions:

- How much do you talk to the lost at a personal level and try to win them to Jesus Christ?
- How far are you prepared to go in your commitment to him?
- How willing are you to be led outside your comfort zone – or do you resent that this could be asked of you?
- Are you rid of all bitterness and grudges – and do you *totally* forgive those who have hurt you (Satan cannot work through a person who is devoid of bitterness and God won't widely use the person who is vindictive)?
- Furthermore, do you dignify every trial God allows – or do you complain and grumble the whole time?
- How much, how regularly and how sacrificially do you give financially to the Lord? And, oh yes, how much do you actually pray every day?

I think of William Cowper's lines:

> Satan trembles when he sees
> The weakest saint upon his knees.
> *William Cowper (1731–1800)*

I sometimes fear that I am not a threat to Satan. Do I want to be? Yes. Think of those people who are a threat to the whole world! I want to be a threat to all that is evil. Our reward at the judgment seat of Christ will not be based on whether we were liked, admired by Christians, built up a good reputation among the saints. Or being famous. I wonder if our reward will be given on the basis whether we were known in hell and were a constant threat to Satan and his fallen angels.

I also believe that those who accomplish great things for God on this planet will be known in hell because they have a reputation in the underworld for being a threat to all of Satan's interests. I would predict that the man or woman who accomplishes the greatest things for God and his kingdom will be unashamed of the Bible generally and the gospel particularly, devoid of bitterness, totally forgiving, full of the love of Christ, sexually pure, fearless in standing for righteousness, unafraid to die for what they believe, self-disciplined, valuing the opinion of God more than people's applause, enjoying intimacy with the Holy Spirit, impervious to the love of money and material things, unable to be bought off or bribed, faithful in prayer, sacrificial and regular in giving of their finances, gentle, continually prepared to move outside their comfort zone – and (last but not least) *known in hell.*

But our comfort zones let us feel at ease day and night, no matter what we do or where we go. We even bring God into everything, supposing he is thrilled. I heard one Hollywood female performer, who goes on stage with the most sensual, provocative dress – with little or nothing on actually say that she prays to God before she faces the audience, and claim that he helps her! In America we have grown accustomed to heavyweight boxers saying, 'Thank you, Lord, for letting me win' after the fight. I myself was once asked to pray for a professional football team in Miami before they went on the field. I did. I knew the other team had a minister praying for them as well. I could have refused, but I took advantage of the ten minutes to preach that they also gave me, then prayed that everyone would have the right attitude – whoever won. I don't know if I did good or harm but I was edging awfully close to Nice God.

Bearing the stigma – the offence – isn't fun. The most truthful thing I think I could say about today's gospel, speaking generally, is that it is de-stigmatised. It seems to me that there is a concerted effort so often when the name of Jesus is uttered to de-stigmatise the gospel.

It is my wish and my sincere prayer that this book will drive us to our knees, move us to seek the face of the God of the Bible; to get to know him and to love him for being exactly as he is – wanting to change nothing about him – and that we will be unashamed of him wherever we go. Peter said that judgment must begin with the family of God (1 Pet. 4:17). If we cannot criticise ourselves we are very insecure indeed. But I suspect that the judgment that is needed is far more than self-criticism but rather a mirroring of God's own feelings regarding the Church that bears his name. He is not happy with it. What follows is an attempt to reveal what I truly believe to be the way God feels at the moment.

1

When God
Plays Hard to Get

'If I were hungry I would not tell you'
Ps. 50:12

It seems to me that the modern Church has drifted so far from the biblical revelation of the true God that any resemblance between him and the popular God of today's generation is quite remote. I think we are in a Romans 1 situation,

> Although they claimed to be wise, they become fools and exchanged the glory of the immortal God for images made to look like mortal man and birds and animals and reptiles. (Rom. 1:22–23)

It is a case in which the God of the Bible is either too holy or too terrible for us; so we have come up with a God that we are comfortable with, at home with, so that we can feel sufficiently religious without having to identify with the ancient God of Israel and the earliest Church.

When I was in seminary I was required to read a book about God 'in an age of atheism'. In this book the author managed to concoct a God whereby one need not be regarded as an atheist after all, even though the God of the Bible was rejected. The theologian Paul Tillich (1886–1965) even suggested that an atheist might be a believer when faith was defined as 'ultimate concern'.

But if you think my own book is an attack on liberalism in the modern Church you would be wrong. I fear that those who deny the historic truths of Holy Scripture are beyond the pale and I seek not very hard to reach them. It is those closer to home that worry me, those who seem to want to hold on to the Bible up to a point but none the less distance themselves from disturbing things we all know are contained in Holy Scripture.

As I said in the Introduction, Ludwig Feuerbach opined that God was nothing more than man's projection upon the backdrop of the universe; that people want to believe in something, especially a God who will take care of them in time of trouble and then give them a home in heaven when they die. Such people mentally project such a God and claim he really does exist. Such a God does not exist of course, says Feuerbach, but he exists in their minds and gives comfort.

It is my view that many Christians do this. They know full well there are things in the Bible they don't want to believe but they are not prepared to throw out everything in the Bible so they fancy a God who approves of their own comfort zone. This God is happy with Christians who reject Bible-denying liberal theology while at the same time approving of their unease with the total revelation of God as revealed in the Old and New Testament. In fact some of these people would go so far as to claim they believe in the whole of the Bible 'from Genesis to maps' – while ensuring that they are at ease in their folk religion. They have been baptised and (in some cases) confirmed; they are (almost certainly) approved of by their church leader; they attend church in varying degrees of regularity and feel quite right indeed in themselves.

What does God himself think of this? Is he so neglected by the masses that he is simply thrilled to have anybody – anywhere – whatever their level of conviction, to give him any attention at all? Is he so hard up or starved for recognition that he will make any measure of concession to any person who makes any effort at all to acknowledge him? Will he therefore show his approval toward any kind of profession of faith because some tipping of the hat toward him is better than nothing?

The nice God of today's religious people might do just that. But not the God of the Bible. Unless he chooses for a while to withhold his real feelings and intentions from us, which is the basis of this chapter.

One reason I abandoned 'Your God is Too Nice' as a title is because I didn't want to make the reader feel guilty or for you to think I feel qualified to judge you. I write out of experience of over fifty years of preaching, most of which have been as a pastor.

If God is too nice, what does this mean? It may mean that he mainly exists in your mind, as we saw when I referred to

17

the German philosopher Feuerbach. Perhaps even you have been worshipping a God you can be comfortable with but who is not the God of the Bible at all. And yet it could mean that the true God has decided to be nice to you for the moment and let you remain in your comfort zone – undisturbed. You might want to say that this isn't being very nice at all if he will eventually show that he was unhappy with me. Yes. But what if he tried for a while but you wouldn't listen? So he let you carry on as if nothing happened. What if he simply decided to be 'nice' to you by letting you remain in your comfort zone and seek a person elsewhere who would indeed listen to him?

Rodney Howard-Browne told me that the Lord put it to him, 'If you don't do what I tell you I will find someone who will.' Jesus said to the church at Ephesus, 'If you do not repent, I will come to you and remove your lampstand from its place' (Rev. 2:5). This is what happens when a church goes astray or soft and God raises up movements to carry on with what ought to have been the Church's own mandate.

Arthur Blessitt, the man who has carried a cross around the world, said that as a student in university he prayed in his dormitory room, 'God, give me a work nobody else will do.'

Someone asked Arthur, 'Why does God speak to you but not to me?'

Arthur replied to the lady, 'Did you ever feel an impulse to speak to someone about Jesus that you didn't know?'

She replied, 'As a matter of fact I have.'

Arthur then said to her, 'Start obeying that voice and it will become clearer and clearer.'

One of the most stunning lines I have come across is in Psalm 50:12: 'If I were hungry I would not tell you.' One evening when our children were sitting on the floor in front of me watching television, not being too interested in what they were watching, I found myself reading that verse. I began to feel very uneasy. I thought to myself, 'I wish the Lord would tell me if he were hungry.' I began to wonder, what if God wanted me to spend more time with him than I had been giving him, would he tell me? I kept reading it, 'If I were hungry I would not tell you.' I couldn't shake it off. I read it again. And again. I began to get the definite feeling that by saying this God was telling me after all he needed and wanted me.

The context of this verse in Psalm 50 is that, though the world is his and although he has cattle on a thousand hills, God is hungry for me. Though he has countless angels – millions and billions – not to mention other people all over the world worshipping him and spending time with him, he wanted me. I seized the moment, for some reason. I decided to fast the next day. I sought his face as I had not done before. The curious thing was, God was hinting the very opposite of what he was saying in Psalm 50:12.

The unveiling of that verse was part of a process that led me to one of the most unusual teachings I have ever come across in Scripture. I have racked my brain many times over what to call it and I still struggle with the best term or phrase for it. I used to call it 'the divine tease'. This was the phrase I used in our School of Theology at Westminster Chapel. This phrase could be defined as God's somewhat playful but deadly serious set-up to let us find out what is in our hearts. It is when he says or does the very opposite of what he intends for us to perceive. But I have since decided to refer to this startling and profound truth as *when God plays hard to get*. For he does! You may say, 'That's not fair.' Perhaps. I still struggle with Jeremiah's words, 'O LORD, you deceived me, and I was deceived' (Jer. 20:7). I don't claim to know all that that means. The theme of this chapter is therefore but the tip of the iceberg of a teaching most extraordinary.

Perhaps the best introduction to this truth is when Jesus was walking with two people – who were kept from recognising who he really was – on the way to Emmaus. It was the same day on which he had been raised from the dead. They came to this village and, when it was time to say good-bye, Jesus 'acted as if he were going further'. This was not his intention at all. He fully intended to stay with them a while longer. He had more to show them. But he did not tell them that and they certainly did not know that. He 'acted' as if he were going further – and he played the role so well that they clearly were going to be upset if he did leave them. The truth is, Jesus wanted them to do exactly as they did – to plead with him to stay on with them. They did not know they were persuading him to do precisely what he planned for them; 'They urged him strongly, "Stay with us, for it is nearly evening; the day is almost over." So [Jesus] went in to stay with them' (Luke 24:29).

When God plays hard to get, then, he often means the very opposite of what he says. And yet it is only because God wants us to plead with him when he appears not to care whether we do or not.

This aspect of God's unusual ways of dealing with us is often in operation when our circumstances suggest it is okay this time to put not God but other things first for the day. If I am so busy, and God knows this, he surely does not expect me to spend time alone with him in praying and reading my Bible. If I am in debt and can't pay my bills he surely does not expect me to return my tithes to him. If there are important people who want to see me he surely would want me to put these people ahead of spending time with ordinary souls. If I did not sleep well last night he understands this and surely would not expect me to try to have my usual quiet time.

Listen to these words from Martin Luther's journal: 'I have a very busy day today. I must spend not two hours, but three, in prayer.' The suggestion might well come to most of us that, given the situation, we need not spend as much time in prayer; but to Luther it meant he must spend more time than ever – to receive divine help to get more done! The movers and shakers and the great saints in church history recognised when God plays hard to get – even if they did not call it that.

Why does God do it? To see what is in our hearts. It is not for him. He already knows. It is for us. It lets us see the truth about ourselves. The truth of this 'side' of God, if I may put it that way, brings out the truth of what we *want*; it brings our true feelings to the surface. The two people on the road to Emmaus had been captivated by Jesus' teaching although they did not have a clue at first it was Jesus. When our hearts burn within us it is a wonderful, wonderful sign that God is at work and wants us to seek his face. The burning heart is there not to mock us but to prod us on to seek his face.

And what do you suppose motivated them then and would do it now for us? You might say, 'If Jesus were there playing hard to get, I would have urged him to stay too – like those two men. They had Jesus himself interpreting Scripture for them. And if he did that with me, I too would plead with him to stay around.' Quite. But they didn't even know it was Jesus. The truth and the application of it is what set their hearts on fire.

It is a strong hint to us that when the truth of the Word of God has this kind of effect on us (Charles Spurgeon used to say to preachers 'When a text gets a hold of you, chances are you have got a hold of it') it is because God himself is at work to draw us closer to him than ever. It is his way of subtly beckoning to us – 'Seek my face.'

Therefore on that night when I kept reading the words, 'If I were hungry I would not tell you', I was gripped and did not know why. It turned out that God was telling me he was yearning for me to spend more time with him. It was a demonstration of God playing hard to get. He does this sort of thing with us. This is one of the reasons he hides his face from us, as he did with Hezekiah: 'God left him to test him and to know everything that was in his heart' (2 Chron. 32:31).

Another time Jesus did this sort of thing was when the disciples were rowing against the wind and waves on the Sea of Galilee. Jesus had gone up into a mountain to pray – and watched the disciples struggling. I have often been fascinated how Jesus did not go at once to help them; he just watched them. Would it not have been nice had Jesus left his place on the mountain at once and turned up on the sea to help them? Or could he not have interceded for them – to ask the Father to stop the wind? But he only watched them.

He does that with all of us. He sees us in our struggle and anxieties – and does not step in. There these disciples were, 'straining at the oars', with Jesus doing nothing to rescue them! He waited until four o'clock in the morning before he showed up. Then when he did so, walking on the water, he was 'about to pass by them' – as if he wasn't even going to identify himself, and they too were kept from recognising him; they thought he was a ghost. But he intervened and said, 'It is I. Don't be afraid' (Mark 6:47–51; cf. Matt. 14:22–27). God is never too late, never too early; he's always just on time.

Jesus did this with the Syro-Phoenician woman. She was not Jewish but Greek, but still approached Jesus and begged him to drive a demon out of her daughter. Jesus treated her with an almost callous coldness. 'First let the children eat all they want,' he told her, 'for it is not right to take the children's bread and toss it to their dogs.' That was enough to put most people off! If the Lord did that with many of us we would walk away in disgust and sarcastically say, 'Thanks a lot – sorry to be such a nuisance to you' – and never know what might have been our lot had we persisted as this woman did. Instead of being offended, acknowledging what would be an insult by today's reckoning and going away in a huff, she reasoned with him: 'Yes, Lord, but even the dogs under the table eat the children's crumbs.' She knew her place and realised Jesus owed her nothing. Then Jesus told you, 'For such a reply, you may go; the demon has left your daughter' (Mark 7:24–30).

There is a widespread feeling among people today that God owes us something, that if we do something that is good or righteous, God should stand to attention and salute us. Our self-righteousness creeps in and we say to ourselves, 'Most people don't even go to church at all. This puts me in a special class; therefore God should be very happy that I am doing this good deed.' This good deed might be anything from attending church, tithing or spending extra time in prayer. We think God should reward those of us who we assume are a cut above most people.

My wife Louise was miraculously healed in 1995 when Rodney and Adonica Howard-Browne laid hands on her and prayed for her. They invited her to come to Lakeland, Florida, to attend the camp meeting there. She agreed to go. On the first night when she walked in, nothing went right. Thousands were there, strange people were doing what seemed to her as very weird things, the people around her were rude where she was sitting. She got up and moved to another area. She wanted to go back to her hotel, pack her bags and get on the next plane to England. But she stayed. She phoned me two days later to say of the camp meeting, 'It is the nearest you get to heaven without dying; it is the greatest experience of my life' (a word I promised myself I would not take too personally). Louise was never to be the same again; those days in Lakeland were more precious than gold. But she had every reason at first to reject everything.

You might think that God would be nice and immediately acknowledge those who sincerely seek his face with a tangible sign on a silver platter. I would have thought he might be nice to Martin Luther the night before he stood before the authorities at Worms, Germany, in the sixteenth century. After all, Luther was standing alone for the gospel – the truth of God's own Word. But Luther walked back and forth in his cell the night before the trial. 'O God, are you dead?' he cried out. No angelic visitation. No congratulations. No sense of God. Only silence. But the next day he uttered those words that changed history: 'Here I stand. I can do no other. God help me. Amen.'

'For my thoughts are not your thoughts, neither are your ways my ways,' declares the LORD. 'As the heavens are higher than the earth, so are my ways higher than your ways and my thoughts than your thoughts.' (Isa. 55:8–9)

God wants us to accept his ways and affirm him as he is, not the way we may want him to be. It is out of our comfort zone where we can learn his ways.

Moses was possibly the greatest leader of men and women in world history. He was a brilliant military strategist. He understood people and their feelings. He had an extremely high degree of patience. He did not take rejection personally. He knew what it was to be loved by his people as well as being hated and rejected. Things were so bad on one occasion that God stepped in and made a deal with Moses. It was a proposition that most leaders I know would have taken with both hands. It was something like this: 'Moses, these people who are supposed to be following you are a sorry lot. I am tired of them as I know you are. Here is what I am going to do: I will destroy them, wipe them off the face of the earth and start all over again with you as the leader.' That is essentially what God said; read it in Exodus 32:9–10 (cf. Num. 14:11–12).

Moses wasted no time in replying to the offer. 'No! It will dishonour your great Name if you do this.'

Then the Egyptians will hear about it! . . . They have already heard that you, O LORD, are with these people and that you, O LORD, have been seen face to face, that your cloud stays over them, and that you go before them in a pillar of cloud by day and a pillar of fire by night. If you put these people to death all at one time, the nations who have heard this report about you will say, 'The LORD was not able to bring these people into the land he promised them on oath; so he slaughtered them in the desert.' (Num. 14:13–16)

Moses then reminded the Lord that he was 'slow to anger, abounding in love' and interceded for the people to be forgiven. Had not Moses been knowledgeable in God's ways – or cared more about his own ego – he would have said 'Yes – kill these unworthy people, Lord.' The psalmist picked up on this event and said, 'So he said he would destroy them – had not Moses, his chosen one, stood in the breach before him to keep his wrath from destroying them' (Ps. 106:23).

It was God playing hard to get. God wanted Moses to respond exactly as he did. But had Moses taken the Lord's words seriously when God said, 'Let's start all over again and I will make a new nation', it would have been because Moses did not know the Lord very well. Moses had developed such a love for the glory of God that his personal feelings and ego were subservient to that honour. Moses did not value his own reputation and esteem; he cared about the way the world thought about the Lord. God also let Moses see for himself that he was getting to know the Lord's very ways. There are not many leaders like Moses. This was the key to his greatness.

God played hard to get in the case of King Saul. But Saul failed to see it and lost the privilege of passing on the kingship to his family. Here is what happened. The prophet Samuel had agreed to be present at a critical time but was overdue for some reason and kept Saul waiting. Nobody knew what was really going on. It was a divine set-up to see what Saul would do. Would the new king honour the word of God? Would he stick to the ways of God as revealed in Scripture or would he presume he was an exception to the revelation of God? Had Saul done what was right he would have said, 'Let us not be hasty. We will wait for Samuel before there is any administering of the burnt offerings because he is the only one the Lord would approve of for this.' If only.

How many of us have done this? In church and during a time of inspiration we may sing 'Have thine own way, Lord' or some devotional hymn by which we pledge to get closer to him. We tell him we want more anointing, that we want to please him in all our ways. Some will go forward at the end of a service and promise the Lord all sorts of things and assume that God applauds such devotion. It is not that he is unimpressed with us at a time like this; he is more interested in how we are in real life a few days later rather than our emotional response at church – however sincere we may have been. God tests our earnestness days or months later – to see how we will react when the divine set-up occurs. We may feel this is not very nice for God to do. But does he not have a right to test our promises?

King Saul's downfall came about because he put himself above the revealed word of God in a time of testing, when the people were quaking with fear because of the Philistines. Samuel set a time at which he would turn up to offer the burnt offerings. When Samuel did not show up as scheduled Saul took it upon himself to offer the burnt offering. The Mosaic Law laid down specific instructions that only a priest – no one else – is authorised to present the burnt offerings (Num. 3:10). But King Saul did it anyway. He explained to Samuel that he felt 'compelled' to do it since Samuel had turned up too late (1 Sam. 13:11–12).

Saul's claim that he felt compelled to do what he did smacks of the behaviour of some people today who fancy that their feelings are an objective basis on which to operate when it comes to the things of God. Some go so far as to say, 'The Lord told me to do this' even though it was blatantly contrary to his own word! To quote Rob Parsons, Christian men who leave their wives often say such things as: 'Darling, we were so young when we got married – we didn't really know what we were doing'; 'In the long run this will be better for you'; 'This will also turn out to be better for the kids'; or 'I've prayed about this – this is fine with God.'

Joseph played hard to get with his eleven brothers when he was prime minister of Egypt. Twenty-two years before they had sold him to the Ishmaelites, never expecting to see him again. It was an awful, cowardly thing to do. The time came when these brothers had to go to Egypt to buy food but did not know it was their brother Joseph they had to face. He had totally forgiven them in his heart and then did something that could be easily misunderstood. When he sent his brothers on their way he secretly put his cup in Benjamin's bag and shortly had Benjamin arrested for stealing his cup! On the surface this seems like a cruel joke. But it was anything but that.

It was a set-up to see whether the brothers had changed in twenty-two years, to find out if they would do to their brother Benjamin (who had replaced Joseph as his father's favourite son) what they had done to Joseph. They had a perfect opportunity to get rid of Benjamin. When Benjamin was found to have Joseph's cup in his bag the brothers could have said, 'Sorry, Benjamin, you are in trouble and you brought this on yourself – you will have to pay for this and remain in Egypt for your crime.' That was what they could have done but they did not do that. They all 'tore their clothes', stood by Benjamin, accompanied him to the prime minister's quarters and pleaded for mercy.

It was a set-up and they passed with flying colours. They had indeed changed. They were not the same jealous brothers who had wanted to get rid of Joseph. Joseph wept when they pleaded for Benjamin's innocence and then revealed to them that he totally forgave them for what they had done twenty-two years before.

Elijah was carrying out this same tactic – playing hard to get – when he kept putting off Elisha. Elisha wanted a double portion of Elijah's anointing – a bold wish. On the day it was known that Elijah would be taken away Elisha doggedly stayed at Elijah's side. Elijah would say to him, 'Stay here; the Lord has sent me to Bethel', but Elisha replied, 'As surely as the Lord lives and as you live, I will not leave you.' Elijah did it again, 'Stay here, Elisha; the Lord has sent me to Jericho.' But Elisha followed Elijah to Jericho. A third time Elijah tried to put Elisha off, 'Stay here; the Lord has sent me to the Jordan.' But Elisha never left his side and was rewarded for his commitment not to let Elijah out of his sight; he received the double portion of Elijah's spirit (2 Kgs. 2:1–15).

For over ten years I have added a petition to my daily prayer list: that I will recognise the exact moment when God is playing hard to get and never miss God's intentions for me. This teaching has profoundly affected my life and outlook and I predict it will have the same effect on you too.

On the night before Jacob was scheduled to meet his brother Esau, an encounter he was dreading, he found himself wrestling with a man all night long. We won't know the details until we get to heaven, but we know this much: at some point during this wrestling match Jacob perceived that this was not an enemy after all who was wrestling with him but a highly valued friend who had power to bless and Jacob was determined not to miss it. It was God playing hard to get. Jacob passed the test – and what a pivotal moment it was for him. Jacob might have run away from the man at first but he kept struggling with him. At some point Jacob got the better of the man – an angel no doubt – and he said to Jacob, 'Let me go, for it is daybreak.' But Jacob replied, 'I will not let you go unless you bless me' (Gen. 32:22–26). The result: Jacob was given a most wonderful compliment from the Lord – would that God would say such to me! For the Lord said to Jacob, 'You have struggled with God and with men and have overcome' (Gen. 32:28). I love the way the Authorised Version puts it: 'For as a prince hast thou power with God and with men, and hast prevailed.'

Martin Luther said that you must know God as an enemy before you can know him as a friend. My old friend Rolfe Barnard used to say to people, 'Don't tell me when you were saved, tell me when you were lost.' What he meant was that a lot of people have assumed they were converted because of a profession of faith but if they did not recall a time when they knew they were lost and in danger of hell, Rolfe reckoned there was reason to question whether such a profession of faith is valid.

Arthur Blessitt tells how he was praying at five o'clock in the morning and God told him to take the cross down from the wall in the coffee shop known as His Place in Hollywood's Sunset Strip and carry it around the world. Arthur sometimes speculates, 'What if I had stopped praying at four o'clock that morning?' (I had assumed he got up early to pray but it was a case of Arthur praying all night.) One could push this point too far of course, but Arthur's point was that he prayed and prayed and the revelation to start carrying the cross was pivotal in his life.

Closely akin to recognising God playing hard to get is breaking the betrayal barrier. This is what every sovereign vessel of God sooner or later must do. There comes a time, puzzling though this may be, when God seems to betray those he loves. It is like when God temporarily left Hezekiah or when Martin Luther felt deserted – when God seemed like an enemy. God still does this! But sadly some people, not knowing God's ways, walk away and never know the blessing that could be theirs had they persevered in a time of struggling and testing. Breaking the betrayal barrier is the spiritual equivalent of science breaking the sound barrier in aviation. It was a great feat but breaking the betrayal barrier is far more productive for the world because through this experience God takes his seasoned servants and uses them to turn the world upside down.

When God told Abraham to leave his own country and come to the land of Canaan where God 'gave him no inheritance . . . not even a foot of ground' (Acts 7:5), he must have felt betrayed. When God told him to sacrifice his son Isaac, he must have felt betrayed. When Joseph refused to sleep with Potiphar's wife but got accused of trying to rape her –

31

and was slammed into prison – he must have felt betrayed by God. After all, for doing the right thing he gets punished! When Moses left Pharaoh's palace but was rejected by his fellow Hebrews, he must have felt betrayed. This list goes on and on. The ultimate sense of betrayal is when Jesus cried out on the cross, 'My God, my God, why have you forsaken me?' (Matt. 27:46); he must have felt betrayed. All these broke the betrayal barrier, and so can we. It comes by never, never, never giving up.

One of the purposes of this book is to show some of God's ways that have been sadly overlooked by us. We learn God's ways by developing intimacy with him, by spending time with him. My wife Louise knows my ways. I know her ways. Habits. Likes. Dislikes. Predictable responses. God yearned for a people who would know him so well that they knew his ways. You may not like the side of him which I have called 'playing hard to get' – one of his ways by which he communicates – but call it a peculiarity, eccentricity or strange part of his personality if you like, that is the way he is.

If God accommodates our ill-posed requests he is being too nice. But he can do that too. I have long been gripped by the Authorised Version rendering of Psalm 106:15: 'And he gave them their request; but sent leanness into their soul.' Sometimes God gives us what we keep demanding despite his warnings, 'This is not best for you' – as when Israel insisted on having a king like other nations. God said to Samuel, 'Listen to all that the people are saying to you; it is not you they have rejected, but they have rejected me as their king' (1 Sam. 8:7). God granted their request. Nice God. For a while. But not for long.

James encourages us when he says, 'You do not have, because you do not ask God' (Jas. 4:2). I like that! But in the next breath he says, 'When you ask, you do not receive, because you ask with wrong motives, that you may spend what you get on your pleasures' (Jas. 4:3). I don't like that. I only wonder to what degree this has applied to me over the years. Is God being nice when he gives us what we want? It would seem so for a while. But not for long.

God is looking for a people who want to know his ways, his heart and his Word so well that they can learn to pray according to his will. I worry about the spirituality of people (however sincere) who are mostly interested in the 'word of knowledge', the 'prophetic word' (or rhema word as it is sometimes called) rather than to know the Bible backwards and forwards. God hears the prayers of those who pray in his will (1 John 5:14) even if they don't always know they are praying in his will. Paul admitted he did not always know if he was praying in God's will but yielded to the Spirit's infallible intercession which is always in God's will (Rom. 8:26–27). We should keep his will before our eyes whenever we pray because this is what is best for us and what we will never regret.

You can therefore make the case that God being nice isn't being so nice after all. Because we will discover at the end of the day that what seemed nice at first wasn't best for us in the long run, and that the cost for such niceness eventually becomes too great to bear. God accommodated our comfort zone for a while – when we thought he was being so good to us – but it is only a matter of time before the sobering truth of his playing hard to get is unveiled.

The problem is that we hastily assume God is being good to

us, answering our prayers and overlooking our superficiality, when the truth is that he is passing us by instead. When we are neither hot nor cold but rather lukewarm we will eventually be spat out of our Lord's mouth (Rev. 3:16). This is the same thing as becoming stone deaf to the Holy Spirit (Heb. 5:13–6:6). Perhaps not today or tomorrow. But it will come.

I therefore use the term 'nice' for what often seems nice for a while. Parents may be regarded as nice because they have too few rules, administer very little discipline or give into their children's wishes as they grow up. But the cost down the road is incalculable. I used to be so resentful of my parents because they made me go to church every time the door was opened, even on Wednesday evenings. I had to stop playing basketball when the kids in the neighbourhood played in my very back yard as I was being hauled off to church. I said, 'Daddy, why can't you be nice like Richard's parents?' The parents of the other kids on our block were so nice. You might like to know that nearly all my old friends – who had such nice parents – either died early deaths in disgrace or ended up as total failures in life.

God has given his Word – the Bible – as the road map for the way he wants the Church to glorify him and the way he wants his children to govern their lives. The slightest deviation may seem so innocent and innocuous at first. But if a jet plane leaving John F. Kennedy airport in New York heading for London is the slightest degree off course only a few miles after take-off, if that deviation is not soon corrected, the same plane seven hours later will be circling over Spain rather than Heathrow.

This book is written lovingly and earnestly as what will

hopefully be a timely caution to a Church that has generally lost its way. I pray that what I write does not come across as moralising or causing any kind of despair or even guilt. But if what I say makes sense to you and you feel God is speaking to you it is a good sign, it seems to me, that God isn't finished with you and there is hope for a bright future.

One way God tests our loyalty and earnestness is to say things we clearly don't understand but which he wants us to take on board none the less. Unfair? Well then, consider Jesus' words, 'Destroy this temple and I will raise it again in three days' (John 2:19). Who understood these words at the time? Nobody, as far as I know – only the Lord himself. This might have been a time for some of his followers to say, 'Count me out – I can't take strange teaching like this.' In any case, those very words were used against Jesus later when, at his trial, one came forward to say, 'This fellow said, "I am able to destroy the temple of God and rebuild it in three days" ' (Matt. 26:61).

Take Jesus' words to a mass audience, 'I tell you the truth, unless you eat the flesh of the Son of Man and drink his blood, you have no life in you. Whoever eats my flesh and drinks my blood has eternal life' (John 6:53–54). You can't get much more offensive than that. Jesus did not bother to explain what he meant by that. He could have said, 'Don't worry – this refers to divine communion after I am ascended to heaven', just as he might have said that the destroying and the raising of the temple referred to his own body (John 2:21). It was part of the playing hard to get syndrome. Most registered their indignation, 'This is a hard teaching. Who can accept it?' And from that time 'many of his disciples turned back and no longer followed him'. For some reason, the Twelve remained. Jesus did ask them, 'You do not want to leave too, do you?' Peter replied, 'Lord, to whom shall we go? You have the words of eternal life' (John 6:60–68). I doubt the Twelve understood what Jesus meant by eating his flesh and drinking his blood any more than those who turned back. But they stayed with him.

There are offensive teachings in the Bible, some of which I have chosen to deal with in this book. God wants us to accept them even if we don't understand them. I don't know of anybody who understands the Trinity, Jesus being God and man simultaneously, the power in the blood of Jesus, why God is gracious and just but lets evil continue, or why he instituted the doctrine of eternal punishment. I never forget Mrs Martyn Lloyd-Jones's observation on the teaching of Hell; she said, 'I just go to Genesis 18:25 – "Will not the Judge of all the earth do right?".' Some reject what they do not like in Scripture and feel God's approval in their comfort zone. God does not disturb them. Not now.

You could say that the central thesis of this book is that there is a sense in which the worst thing that can happen to us is for God to be nice, to let us stay comfortable where we are – and never arouse us to leave our comfort zones. If God being nice means that he graciously steps down and rescues us from our blindness and bondage, then may he ever be nice to us. But the worst thing is when he backs off from us, appearing to be nice. He just lets us be. Perhaps the way it was said of Ephraim, who was joined to idols: 'Leave him alone!' (Hos. 4:17). Those who would not accept the revelation of God – whether by creation or through conscience – were not struck down by lightning or brought to their knees by thunder; we read that

God merely 'gave them over' to their desires and to minds void of judgment (Rom. 1:24, 26, 28).

What is described in Romans 1 does not directly describe the believer but the person who rejects the light of God on their conscience. But this truth is paralleled none the less when true believers foolishly say, 'I wish God would leave me alone.' Be careful or he may do just that. When a believer was sleeping with his stepmother – and would not take godly counsel at first – the apostle Paul ordered such a person to be handed over to Satan, 'so that the sinful nature may be destroyed and his spirit saved on the day of the Lord' (1 Cor. 5:5). Though extreme we know God can deal with his own people like this. '"The Lord will judge his people." It is a dreadful thing to fall into the hands of the living God' (Heb. 10:30–31).

I don't want that to happen to you or to me. And yet I want him to correct me if this is what I need.

2

The Comfort Zone

'It is the nature of man as he grows older . . . to protest against change, particularly change for the better'

John Steinbeck

If you read my book *The Anointing* you may recall the chapter entitled 'Moving outside Your Comfort Zone'. If you want an increase in your anointing, and if you go where the anointing is to be found, you will almost certainly be required to move outside your comfort zone.

The comfort zone is like being at home. It is like being with family, your loved ones. You are at ease. You are not threatened. You are in the company of the familiar. You've been there before. It is peaceful. It may not be the supernatural peace that transcends understanding that is promised in Philippians 4:7, but it is peace none the less; it is what I would call natural peace, or peace at the natural level. It does not cross your mind to question or be afraid. You are, simply, comfortable in this state.

I grew up in Ashland, Kentucky. It was a town of 29,000 people. I walked to school every day with neighbourhood kids who were like family. I didn't realise then of course how precious the days were or how happy I was. A few years ago I took my family back to Ashland. As we drove into the little town the sign that let you know you were within the city limits said, 'Ashland, population 29,000'. Forty years later the population was the same! That made me feel I was getting back into my comfort zone straight away.

But that feeling ended there. Nothing else was the same. We drove to my old home on Hilton Avenue. The present owners had changed everything. The house next door was altogether different. We drove up and down Hilton Avenue where I had delivered the *Ashland Daily Independent* – our local newspaper – each afternoon when I came home from school. Almost all the homes were different. We drove to the school I first attended when I was six years old. It had changed. We went to the school where I attended after then and it had been torn down. I went to see Coles Junior High – the building was no longer a school; so too Ashland High School. What used to be 'downtown' was almost like a ghost town; most shops were now to be found in a large shopping mall. Even my old church had had a face lift and the auditorium inside was hardly recognisable.

When I came to Ashland, I wanted to go back home. I couldn't. As a saying goes, 'You can't go back home.'

Since writing most of this chapter Louise and I have driven up to Miami from our home in Key Largo to attend the annual

'Cuba Nostalgia' exhibition. Shortly after we married in 1958 we made a couple of trips to Havana, Cuba, and fell in love with that beautiful country as well as certain types of Cuban music. We have owned dozens of records of Cuban music, which we have played over the years, and we enjoyed much the same atmosphere at the exhibition. We drank Cuban coffee, ate Cuban food, enjoyed talking with Cubans who miss their country and heard Cuban music all over the place. There was nothing spiritual about it – it was wholly nostalgic.

And yet I have often suspected that some people choose a type of ministry, church leader, church or church service not because it is truly Spirit-filled or theologically sound but because it gives a nostalgic feeling of being at home, what they are used to or hope somehow to recapture. Nostalgia – though we are not always conscious that is what it really is – is perhaps a synonym for comfort zone. I am perhaps the worst for wanting this.

But many want to go back home, and a lot of us continue to try. I do it with food. I love to eat. It is one of life's greatest pleasures for me. I tend to try to recapture tastes I remember as a child, like the way my grandmother fried chicken or cooked green beans. But she went to heaven many years ago and her recipes and way of cooking went with her. Perhaps she cooks for the angels! After marrying, Louise and I used to order a pizza in Fort Lauderdale that exceeded any I had ever eaten. When we were away from Florida that pizza parlour closed down and never relocated, and I still long for a pizza like theirs. It will never happen.

When we made the decision to retire, various friends warned us that we would find some difficulty in settling into America.

'Don't you believe it', I said. Although I knew we would miss England I was so sure it would be good to go home and live in Florida where we had lived before, the land of fishing and sunshine. But, strange as it may seem to you, we have been out of our comfort zone from the moment we arrived. Nothing was like it was, only the good weather. As for fishing, I did more of it when I was minister of Westminster Chapel because we could come to Florida for six weeks each summer and I myself would do almost nothing but fish. Now that we live in Key Largo, right on Largo Sound with a little boat waiting for me, for some reason, I do so little fishing. Nothing is like it was.

It is one thing to choose to go outside your comfort zone; quite another to find yourself outside your comfort zone involuntarily. However much you try to like where you are now or do what you used to do, you are simply outside your comfort zone. You want things to be like they used to be and nothing is the same.

Being outside your comfort zone is not fun. You are uneasy. You yearn for the familiar. You want what will make you feel good – naturally. Seeking one's comfort zone is one of the most natural things in the world to do. And yet if at the natural level you cannot always stay in your comfort zone, how much more is this true at the spiritual level.

As I said, God almost always requires his servants to move outside their comfort zone. Read Hebrews 11, the 'faith chapter' of the Bible. There is a common thread that runs right through the chapter and characterises each person who did what they did by faith; they all had to move outside their comfort zone and not a single one of them had the luxury of repeating what had been done before them. For it is easy to do what you know has been done before, where there is a precedent for what you are doing; because it is safe.

In C.S. Lewis's *The Lion, the Witch and the Wardrobe* are the unforgettable lines:

'Ooh!' said Susan . . . 'Is he – quite safe? I shall feel rather nervous about meeting a lion.'

'That you will, dearie, and no mistake,' said Mrs Beaver; 'if there's anyone who can appear before Aslan without their knees knocking, they're either braver than most or else just silly.'

'Then he isn't safe?' said Lucy.

'Safe?' said Mr Beaver; 'Don't you hear what Mrs Beaver tells you? Who said anything about safe? 'Course he isn't safe. But he's good. He's the King, I tell you.'

God isn't safe. But he's good. We must never forget this when outside our comfort zone but in God's will. God wants only what is best for us. When we are directed by the Holy Spirit to be outside our comfort zone, it is always for our good.

For example, Noah 'walked with God', following in the steps of Enoch who 'walked with God' (Gen. 5:22; 6:9). So far, so good. They both did the same thing. For all I know Noah may have thought that what happened to Enoch would happen to him if he followed Enoch's example in walking with God. As for Enoch, he was taken to heaven one day (Gen. 5:24; Heb. 11:5). As for Noah, he might have wondered each day if he was doing something wrong because he was still around! But God had different plans for Noah. He was told one day to build an ark and with it came specific instructions (Gen. 6:14ff.). He might have thought, 'I'd far prefer to be taken to heaven since I am walking with God as Enoch did.' But no. Furthermore, he obeyed and 'moved with fear' in doing so (Heb. 11:7, AV), thus being outside his comfort zone. Can you imagine the stigma Noah and his family must have experienced as they erected that ark – a thing unprecedented in history and which must have made them the laughing-stock of the people?

Maybe Abraham wondered if he too would get to build an ark, for by this time the idea of building an ark was surely de-stigmatised since Noah had been thoroughly vindicated. Even though God promised he would never again destroy the whole earth by water, building arks none the less might have been seen by some as the wave of the future and the evidence you were obedient to God. Noah, however, was the first and the last person to be required to build an ark. What if God leads you to do what is unprecedented and which will not be repeated? Can you live with this? Can you accept this? As for Abraham, he found himself outside his comfort zone by not even knowing 'where he was going' (Heb. 11:8) or even receiving specific instructions exactly what to do! And what a lacklustre legacy he left for Isaac and Jacob; they with Abraham 'lived in tents' (Heb. 11:9), hardly the most comfortable way of living.

Moses was brought up in the opposite standard of living of the patriarchs – living in luxury and royal privilege, but he refused to be known as the son of Pharaoh's daughter and 'chose to be ill-treated along with the people of God rather than to enjoy the pleasures of sin for a short time' (Heb. 11:24–25). This could not have been an easy decision. And yet he 'regarded disgrace for the sake of Christ as of greater value than the treasures of Egypt' (Heb. 11:26). But he was outside his comfort zone.

Hebrews 11:32 refers to Samuel. He was instructed by God to anoint David to be king when there already was a king! Indeed, Samuel wanted to argue with the Lord on this call: 'How can I go? Saul will hear about it and kill me' (1 Sam. 16:2). But he had to go where the anointing of the Spirit was present and to find tomorrow's man.

The list in Hebrews 11 goes on and on, even leaving out stalwarts in the Old Testament who could be mentioned. Every single one that God mightily used, sooner or later, had to move outside their comfort zone. However, all these did what they did voluntarily. They did what they did by faith; they chose to obey the Holy Spirit. They willingly went outside their comfort zone.

They were truly great men and women who did this. Shakespeare said, 'Some people are born great, some achieve greatness and some have greatness thrust upon them.' The people described in Hebrews 11 achieved greatness and it was precisely because they willingly went outside their comfort zone. So will you, not necessarily in the eyes of people but in the eyes of him who will one day look at you and say, 'Well done'. God wants all of us to experience this.

And yet there is such a thing as having the uneasiness of being outside your comfort zone thrust upon you. It is not what you sought, certainly not what you yearned for. But before you knew it, there it was. Perhaps it was suddenly being in an awkward situation in the office. Maybe you were in a strange service at church, or heard a sermon that made you feel uncomfortable. It may have been an unwelcome knock at your front door. You may have been put on the spot by someone who claimed to be telling you what they thought was for your good. Or you might have just received unhappy results of any examination and your future seems bleak. It isn't fun.

This is not to say, then, that being outside your comfort zone is always and necessarily good! Let no one think that being outside your comfort zone is always a sign of the anointing, evidence of your obedience or proof you are pleasing God. It could be the opposite. God has created us with an in-built preservation instinct that keeps us from going too close to the edge of a cliff, driving too fast down the motorway or walking in an area barefooted where there may be snakes and scorpions. I never worried about walking about at night as a boy in Ashland, Kentucky; but I would not feel the same way today, much less walking alone in Miami at night, just 50 miles north of where we now live – and some places there in broad daylight.

There is a natural fear that is God-given: of not taking precautions when you know there could be danger, of not preparing for an exam when your future is at stake, of eating wrong foods or too much of what may be healthy in moderation. Indeed, psychologists speak of 'creative anxiety'. Whereas anxiety may be seen as the common denominator of all psychopathology there is also an anxiety that can lead to getting things done, that guides one to wonderful inventions and new ideas that change the world for good.

So do not think that merely being outside your comfort zone is always good. It could be harmful and very bad for you indeed. The devil might even make an overly conscientious person move outside their comfort zone and cause them to end up in bewilderment, disillusionment, depression or unbelief. For example, I have known some sincere Christians to do foolish things – such as taking all their savings and giving the money away to an unscrupulous preacher; or spending all their time in the work of their church, neglecting their children and letting their marriages break down; or even giving too much time in fasting and prayer – and get weak and tired – when they needed to be physically on top and conscientious about their secular jobs.

My favourite line in Shakespeare is: 'To thine own self be true.' These words are not in the Bible as far as I know but the gist of them is – throughout Proverbs and particularly what Paul is saying in Romans 14, especially verse 9 to which I will return below. And I have learned that the Holy Spirit will not lead you to go against Scripture or make you do what gives you an uneasy, unsettled feeling within. Remember throughout the reading of this book this principle that you can hang on to: the Holy Spirit will never lead you to be untrue to yourself or to violate your conscience.

The problem is, when you are found outside your comfort zone it is of course unsettling. And if you push this point too far we will all have an excuse to stay in our comfort zones forever. Many things I myself have had to do over the years, having to leave my comfort zone, made me uneasy at first and were very unsettling indeed.

When I first heard of the 'Kansas City prophets' (as they were then called) I hit the ceiling! Not only did these men take me out of my comfort zone, I found myself in 'alarm bells' zone. The more I heard in those early days, the more I felt I must roll up my sleeves and warn my friends about these 'occultic' men. Talk about being outside my comfort zone! But I was wrong. In a few months I climbed down and found myself having to make a hard decision – whether to be involved with some of them. One or two became close friends. I did and have been thankful ever since. But I was outside my comfort zone. At first.

What is outside your comfort zone today may be the very centre of your comfort zone tomorrow. This is because once you obey and get used to the scariness of being outside your comfort zone it begins to seem like home. Before long you may have to move yet again and go to the unknown, like Abraham who went out but did not know where he was going.

My point is this. Whether it be an unusual ministry or a different theological point of view, an initial uneasiness is what we all tend to feel when outside our comfort zone. We can choose to say, 'This is like walking the streets of Miami at night' and stay away, or ask whether the Holy Spirit, just maybe, could be leading us on to a greater anointing of the Spirit than we have ever known in our lives.

How then do we know we are outside our comfort zone but still in God's perfect will? I will now share an acrostic that has served me well over the years and one which I have shared with the members of Westminster Chapel many times – both from the pulpit and in the vestry. It is based upon an acrostic, P – E – A – C – E. Consider asking these questions when you are not sure what to do.

Providential

Is it providential? Do things 'happen' or do you have to break a door down in order to get through it? If you have to force a door open or nudge the arm of Providence, be careful: you are about to enter a realm outside your comfort zone, yes, but not a realm that is accompanied with the peace of God. If things happen without your manipulation, proceed. But if you have played 'man the manipulator' and made things happen to suit your wishes, stop. God almost certainly is not behind what you are trying to do.

Enemy

What would your enemy – the devil – want you to do? I often ask this: what would Satan want me to do at this point? Figure it out – it probably won't be very hard – and do the opposite. Most of us have a fairly shrewd idea what the devil would want us to do: cheat, hate, have sex outside of marriage, go deeply into debt, boast about our accomplishments, give into jealousy, gossip, point the finger, hold the grudge. Do the opposite and you will almost certainly get it right.

Authority

What does the Bible say? That is your supreme and infallible authority for faith and conduct. You will never improve on Holy Scripture. The way to know the will of God begins with knowing the Bible well. It is entirely God-breathed (2 Tim. 3:16) and therefore written by the Holy Spirit (2 Pet. 1:21).

You therefore should ask whether there is a biblical warrant for what you are thinking of doing or embracing. If it is not validated by Scripture, stop at once. No need to proceed to the next premiss. God will never lead you to do that which clearly goes against his own Word.

Confidence

When I am the most sure I am in the will of God I am the most confident. When I know I am obedient, that I am doing what I have a mandate to do, I feel confident through and through. A Greek word for this is *parresia*. It means 'boldness'. It is sometimes translated 'plainly' (John 10:24). It was what Peter experienced when he preached on the day of Pentecost (Acts 2:29). It is a good, good feeling. But when I lose this it is often a signal something has gone wrong. God wants you to feel confident.

Ease

In your heart of hearts do you feel ease? Are you troubled or unsettled? Be very, very careful. From my own experience, even when I am scared and conscious that I am taking a hard decision but have peace inside, I am seldom disappointed when I proceed. When we announced my decision to retire from Westminster Chapel, having been there for twenty-five years, I had times of near panic – 'What ever am I doing? I am giving up security. Leaving when they are begging me to stay. Why would I do this?' I only know I had peace in my heart of hearts.

For this acrostic to be a safe guide for you, all five of those points must come together. If only four are true, that is still not enough. To have PEACE we need all of them. But if all five are there, I can safely promise you it will be a positive and happy way forward.

Yes, 'To thine own self be true.' I now come to Romans 14:19, the verse that is the foundation for my acrostic above. Paul told us we must do the things that make for peace. 'Let us therefore make every effort to do what leads to peace and to mutual edification' (Rom. 14:19). The peace that I have in mind in the above acrostic is internal – the ease we feel within – but Paul also has in mind what leads to peace with others, remembering of course that he previously said: 'If it is possible, as far as it depends on you, live at peace with everyone' (Rom. 12:18). We will always have those who do not want to make peace with us. But we must try.

The question we now must attempt to answer is: how do you know when being outside your comfort zone is of the Holy Spirit and when is it your own doing? In my book *The Anointing* I have a chapter entitled 'The Limits of Our Anointing', where I make the case that we all must accept the limits of our anointing. Nobody can do everything. King Saul's downfall began when he went outside his anointing. As we saw above, because he was king he thought he was above the Word of God and also could go outside his calling, including offering the burnt offering – an act only a priest was allowed to do. But Saul did just that. 'You acted foolishly', Samuel told him, and then prophesied that he would be replaced by a man after God's own heart (1 Sam. 13:9–14).

It takes a lot of humility (and sometimes courage) to

recognise the limits of your anointing and never to go outside that anointing. This principle is based partly on Romans 12:3: 'Do not think of yourself more highly than you ought, but rather think of yourself with sober judgment, in accordance with the measure of faith God has given you.' I have to accept the limits of my intelligence, my gifting and my calling. I must not try to be somebody else or imitate another's gift or anointing. God made you you and when he made you he threw the mould away. He wants each of us to accept ourselves as we are and be content with the way he made us and with our particular calling.

King Saul's problem was he wasn't content with his calling. You would have thought that being king would be enough! No. He wanted more. He took himself too seriously and it led to his downfall. We therefore must accept the limits of our gifting but also our mandate – and not transgress by crossing over a line by which we go outside that calling.

I have been given an opportunity to talk with certain leaders in the Middle East, among them Yasser Arafat. It is an honour to be invited into the presence of a head of state and have lunch with them, regardless of whether you agree with everything they have stood for. But political leaders, understandably, want to talk politics. I have had to make it clear to Arafat that my role is theological and non-political. I have said to him: 'I do not come to you as a political leader but as a follower of Jesus Christ. I come as a man of prayer.' But the Palestinian leaders, sitting around that long table in Ramallah, will still bring up political issues. I have had to force myself to avoid delving into politics but live within my calling: to pray and talk about Jesus Christ.

The funny thing is, going into politics with Israeli and Palestinian leaders would be widening my comfort zone. I happen to love politics. Ninety per cent of my television-watching is political news. I have some fairly strong political views. I do not make them public and not even private if I thought somebody might quote me. Therefore to concentrate on politics would be right in the middle of my comfort zone. But to avoid politics, especially if I can please those around me when I am with political leaders, is to go outside my comfort zone – which I am required to do.

The irony is, staying with your calling is in a sense to stay in your comfort zone because this is where you have maximum peace. But there is always the time – it will come sooner or later – when you know you have to go outside your comfort zone, but never outside your calling, to keep that peace.

To put it another way: how do I know when I am being cautious and prudent by refusing to be found outside my comfort zone? How do I know when it is a natural but reasonable fear that keeps me where I am? How do I know this fear is not a fear of displeasing the Lord? I answer: when pride is at stake. It is commonly called 'the fear of man' – what people will think or say. This fear is the chief ingredient that keeps us in our comfort zone and thus militates against our discovering God's ways.

These words keep coming to me – again and again: 'They have not known my ways' (Ps. 95:10; Heb. 3:10) – stated in anger but none the less with lament and sorrow. God's heart ached when he said, 'I was grieved with that generation'; namely, that ancient generation of Israel that might have inherited the Promised Land but forfeited it. This is the way

God feels about us when we shrink back and reject the offer he makes to us, the way he has revealed himself to us and the things he has asked us to do. He wants us to know his ways. He yearns for us to know what he is like and love him for being just as he is.

The greatest thing one's husband or wife wants to hear from the other is: I love you just the way you are. It is so affirming to be fully accepted as we are. God wants that from us. He wants us to know him, see exactly what he is like and the way he is – he calls it 'my ways'. The thing is, you might not like his ways. You may dislike his ways – intensely, for all I know. But the point is, God wants us to know his ways and love him just as he is. The problem with Israel was, they did not even know his ways. This made him sad. But also angry.

God therefore wants us to know him so well that what he does, does not take us by surprise. For those who do not know his ways there will be a reaction – 'This cannot be God' – when he chooses to manifest himself in a manner that finds us outside our comfort zone.

Is your mind made up as to what God is like? How do you know whether your perception of God is little or no different from that of Feuerbach, who said that God is nothing more than our projection upon the backdrop of the universe? For if our minds are made up we will never know what it would have been like had we the courage to overcome fear and thus explore the awesome things about God that he wants to show us.

This book is designed to warn us and, if possible, to catch us in time so that we will discover after all (before it is too late) what God wants us to see about him. We need not be like the comfortable majority who opt for the familiar.

The question is: when is it a black-or-white situation (to sin or not to sin) and when is it a grey-area situation – when you are not displeasing God? The answer: when God clearly calls for you to move outside your comfort zone – as he did with Noah, Abraham, Moses or Samuel. When God clearly taps you on the shoulder then move is what you and I must do; we have no choice but to obey. Otherwise we forfeit the blessing of the Holy Spirit and risk the unthinkable – not hearing God speak again to us and becoming stone deaf to the Holy Spirit (Heb. 5:11–6:6 – elaborated on in my book *Are You Stone Deaf to the Spirit?*).

I had a hard decision to make shortly after Arthur Blessitt visited us at Westminster Chapel in 1982. Not only did I have to decide whether to continue what he started (chorus singing, the altar call, witnessing on the streets) or go back to business as usual; but I also had to decide in those days whether I was led by the Holy Spirit to turn Westminster Chapel into a charismatic church. Some may think we did become a charismatic church then. We did not. The proof of this is that I had many charismatic leaders (whom I respected a lot) who urged me to press on with what we began. The big question those days was whether I was taking the Chapel too fast or too slow – or just right. I was under a little pressure to do things 'charismatic' but I never felt right about it. I had no mandate from the Holy Spirit.

True, what was begun under Arthur's influence seemed very charismatic to some. But pressing on with a certain style and exercising all the 'gifts of the Spirit' in the services would take us even further outside our comfort zone – which some pleaded with me to do. But I did not accept their advice. We went at our own pace. Some thought we moved too fast; some not fast enough.

I chose a comfort zone this time. We kept at a pace that, it seemed to me, was right for our people who by and large had no background whatever in things 'charismatic' but only reformed thinking. You could say I gave into a weakness – not wanting to displease certain people more than I had done already. I barely kept the old battleship afloat as it was! And yet some have lovingly argued with me that I would have done far better to ignore all critics and followers and just 'go for it' regardless of the consequences. I could have done so and would have done it to glorify God. But I just did not have the intestinal fortitude to do so. I would admit that I gave in to a weakness. I do not believe I sinned, however.

Did Moses sin when he gave in to the people to allow divorce? See Deuteronomy 24:1–4. Jesus said that Moses 'permitted you to divorce your wives because your hearts were hard. But it was not this way from the beginning' (Matt. 19:8). Those words 'it was not this way from the beginning' indicate that Moses would have been quite right never to allow divorce. But he gave into the people. Was this Moses' comfort zone? I think it could have been. Did he sin by giving into them? No. He apparently did this without displeasing God. And yet I think too that God was being nice.

I can recall other situations in Westminster Chapel when I opted for the comfort zone – in weakness. There were occurrences that emerged in my final year to which I will refer. I announced my retirement thirteen months in advance to give them good time to make the transition after having me since 1977. I still hoped revival would come during the final year. I took a lot of risks but I also gave into a weakness – twice.

The first of these was when I found out that Mahesh Chavda was free to hold an all-night prayer meeting for us at Westminster Chapel. This had been an aspiration of mine ever since some of our people, including Louise, had attended one of Mahesh's all-night prayer meetings in west London. I was so thrilled that he had a time when he could do it. I took advantage of it with both hands. I announced it publicly. Many were as thrilled as I was. But the next day our chapel manager told me that we must not do this as he had recently sent out a letter to the surrounding neighbours promising them that we would never have a service after ten o'clock at night. This came about because neighbours had complained about loud music that had occurred late one Saturday evening when a certain charismatic group of people had asked to use the Chapel for the day. Our chapel manager had promised this would never happen again.

I could have overruled. I had not written the letter and had not asked him to write it, although what he did was a reasonable thing to do. But I could have said, 'Sorry, I promised Mahesh and the people we will do this. Besides we want to be open to the Holy Spirit and pray for revival.' I could have let the neighbours complain again, or I might have asked the people who attended the all-night prayer meeting to be as quiet as possible although we would certainly have been heard by neighbours at three o'clock in the morning. I gave in, yielded to a comfort zone. I did not want to offend anybody in my final year at the Chapel. I phoned Mahesh, who graciously understood. But I have wondered many times what might have happened had we proceeded with that all-night prayer meeting.

The other incident has worried me more. I began an era of spontaneous singing at the Chapel during the partaking of the Lord's Supper. Usually after the bread and wine were served to those present, I would begin singing – making up the words as we went along . . . 'We praise you, Lord . . . we love your name . . . we honour you . . . welcome Holy Spirit . . .' This was done without any musical accompaniment and yet we sang on key together. The sound was glorious as the congregation joined in. Sometimes the Spirit would come down in great power. Some people would laugh, some would groan. Some would fall off the pews into the floor. It was one of the most memorable eras of my whole twenty-five years there. But some of the church were not pleased. I gave in rather than allow for the possibility of a big blow-up just before we retired.

I do not believe I sinned in either of these incidents. But I gave in to weakness none the less. I am not thrilled with my decisions. I like to think, just maybe, it was comparable to Paul escaping the Damascenes – which he called a weakness (2 Cor. 11:30–33). He was not thrilled with what he did and I still think a lot about giving in to my own weakness on these occasions because I did not want to cause trouble in the Chapel at this juncture.

There is one further aspect to the comfort zone syndrome which I must address in this chapter. I refer now to the way our perception of comfort zone changes according to our being 'in season, out of season'. 'In season' is when the full tide of a spiritual wave has set in and powerfully washes away – or hides

– the debris that had been visible on the shoreline. When the Holy Spirit is present in power things do not tend to bother us very much, upset us or even threaten us as they did before. The Spirit makes our problems disappear!

When I first had the vision of the Pilot Light ministry at the Chapel which led to our street witnessing, nothing could have stopped me from being out on the steps of the Chapel to witness to passers-by that first Saturday in June 1982. I would have done it alone. Several did join me as it turned out, but I was so full of assurance of the Spirit – I had a rugged boldness and freedom that I had not known before – that I would have gladly appeared like a fool, handing out tracts and talking to people about Jesus Christ all by myself.

But a year or two later the tide began to ebb its way out. The excitement diminished. Many who had started out with us stopped coming out on Saturday mornings. The number of people praying to receive Christ came to nearly zero – week after week. I didn't feel like going out any more. I could use those Saturdays to better advantage. This was the way I felt. When I first went with Arthur I was out of my comfort zone. But in a short period of time I was at home with this – full of confidence and with a sense of God on me. But I realised later on that I was now out of my comfort zone again. Nothing came to fruition as I had hoped. Revival certainly had not come. We were not reaching many people that we knew of.

In a word: to remain a Pilot Light and keep this ministry going by that time was again to go outside my comfort zone. I eventually went through four stages:

1   out of my comfort zone (when I first started witnessing on the streets);

2   in my comfort zone (once I felt the Lord powerfully with me);

3   out of my comfort zone (when I realised nothing great was happening as a result of our faithful witnessing every Saturday). I might add that trouble was brewing within the membership that began with Arthur Blessitt's ministry to us. A move was on in the membership to get rid of me. I no longer had Arthur at my side. He was out of the picture and I had to decide what to do from now on. The baton had passed to me. I made a decision and went through to the next stage;

4   not to slip back into my comfort zone but to remain outside my comfort zone and be there every Saturday – whether many joined me or if people were converted. I simply kept it up.

A few years later Benjamin Chan started a prayer meeting on Saturday mornings to uphold us before the Lord while we were on the streets. We did not do one thing differently but we noticed a dramatic increase in numbers of people who prayed to receive Christ. The Pilot Light ministry began to flourish. It continues to this day. I never missed a Saturday during the final twenty years of my ministry in London unless I was out of town.

My point is this. When the Spirit subsides and ebb tide comes – which always seems to happen – we find ourselves outside our comfort zone again. This is because the Holy Spirit at first makes us comfortable in the very sphere we once dreaded. But then he tests us – to see what we will do during ebb tide. This is why Paul admonished that we be 'instant' whether in season or out of season (2 Tim. 4:2, AV). Therefore when there is a diminishing in the measure of the Spirit's assurance and comfort and the tide goes out, the debris and all sorts of things that were on the shoreline (but covered over) become obvious – and obstacles loom large. We then must make the choice to please God indeed by doing what we know is right even if we don't feel like doing it – whether quiet time praying, reading your Bible every day, witnessing, tithing and any number of things which become tedious and boring, if not sheer drudgery, when God hides his face.

When the tide is in it is easier to do the things we know we ought to do – like total forgiveness, dignifying the trial, witnessing to the lost, turning the cheek (Matt. 5:39), accepting an injustice (1 Cor. 6:7), or not taking oneself so seriously. The problem with the old spiritual, 'Every time I feel the Spirit moving in my heart I'll pray', is that when the Spirit is moving in your heart it is like the comfort zone! It's easy to pray and do all the things I just referred to.

True spirituality is present when you don't feel the Spirit moving in your heart – but you pray anyway. It is like going outside your comfort zone when you carry out obedience but do not feel like doing it. But this pleases God and honours him no end.

The Holy Spirit is depicted in the New Testament as a dove – a very shy, sensitive bird. As I say in my book *Sensitivity of the Spirit*, pigeons and doves are in the same family but they are none the less quite different from each other. Doves are gentle, afraid of people, peaceful and easily scared and chased away. When Paul said, 'Do not grieve the Holy Spirit of God' he used a word in the Greek that means 'to get your feelings hurt'. Because the Holy Spirit, a very sensitive person, gets his feelings hurt – easily – but never lets on that he is offended. When the Dove lifts from us we don't feel a thing. We just carry on as if nothing happened, often realising long afterwards that we offended the Spirit. It is like the oft-repeated statement, 'If the Holy Spirit were completely withdrawn from the Church today, ninety per cent of the work of the Church would continue on as if nothing happened.'

In much the same way the Holy Spirit flutters away and leaves us to ourselves and we continue on without him, like Joseph and Mary, who went a day's journey without Jesus, thinking he was right there with them (Luke 2:43–44). It is scary to realise that this continues to happen. God unobtrusively slips away from us and we feel nothing – often thinking the Lord is with us as much as ever. We get accustomed to existence without his powerful, conscious presence and begin to think we are still being led by him.

Now to what is perhaps the most important point yet. When the Spirit is not powerfully present – for whatever reason the tide is out – we tend to make critical decisions in that state which are dictated by the flesh not the Spirit, but we may think it is the Spirit! Because the Holy Spirit tends to diminish in measure not all at once – like the ebbing tide – we move back into the old comfort zone and do not realise we are vulnerable to fleshly decisions, choices we would not make were we to be filled with the Spirit.

For example, once we make the decision to forgive someone

totally, it is an act of our will, and yet it is done through the supernatural power of the Holy Spirit. But later on we often begin to say to ourselves, 'It is not right that this person I have forgiven is not caught and found out.' We get upset. If we are not careful we will slip into the old comfort zone that justifies the anger and the grudge. What are we to do? There is only one answer: move outside your comfort zone again – and forgive them.

But when the Spirit wanes, and he usually does, we are liable to make fleshly decisions. We think at the time our judgments are sound, solid and spiritual but they may not be at all. As for total forgiveness, it is one of the hardest things in the world to maintain. 'The heart is deceitful above all things, and desperately wicked: who can know it?' (Jer. 17:9, AV). The very people we once forgave we begin holding a grudge against all over again if we are not careful.

So too with the way we react to a manifestation of the Holy Spirit. When we are full of the Spirit and walking in the Spirit we will not miss what God is doing when the Spirit manifests – whether through crying or laughing or falling on the floor. But when we are in the flesh we find this sort of thing disgusting and reprehensible. And fancy that we have spiritual discernment! I know. I've been there!

Many of us miss what God is in because we fancy ourselves to be competent and spiritual judges of what is happening when in fact we may have become lukewarm and smug. Our comfort zones can masquerade as the witness of the Spirit when it is really a case of the tide being out and our having very little authentic discernment. In this state God is nice – at least for a while. He lets us do what we want to do. We may later say, 'God, why did you let me stay like that? Why didn't you open my eyes?'

And what is the answer to questions like these? The answer comes from the niceness of God in painlessly letting us off the hook, moving on without us when we didn't pick up on his subtle wooing, or leaving us alone when we were smug and unteachable. Perhaps he waits for a time in which we will be in a fit state to listen to him.

What follows in these chapters are what I believe to be what the God of the Bible is like and the way we should perceive the truth of God and the Spirit of God. It is when the tide is fully in, when it is in season with us, that we can grasp what he is like and love him for being the way he is. It is the way we would see things were we to leave our comfort zones purely out of obedience and for his glory.

I don't mean to be unfair, but if we find some of what follows to be offensive, it may be blindness that keeps us comfortable in that state rather than the way we would see things were we to be wide awake and keeping in step with the Holy Spirit. Or, dare I say it, the way we will all see things one day.

If you are by chance spiritually asleep, like the foolish virgins (Matt. 25:1–5), you will probably not like a lot of what follows in this book. There are three things you probably already know about sleep:

1   we don't know we are asleep until we wake up;
2   we do things in our dreams we would not do wide awake; and
3   we hate the sound of an alarm.

This book is designed to sound an alarm – to help us see for ourselves whether our comfort zone is a benign 'grey' area, or if it is a case of God graciously arousing us from slumber – from our perception of Nice God to seeing the God of the Bible. If he so arouses us he is being more than nice but awesome and merciful indeed. May the Holy Spirit guide you by the hand as we take a look at the true God.

He's not safe. But he is good.

Moreover, it can be the crucial test whether God means more to you and me than anything or anyone else.

3

The Fear and Jealousy
of God

'I don't think anything has been done in the name of Christ
and under the banner of Christianity that has proven more
destructive to human personality, and hence counterproductive
to the evangelistic enterprise, than the un-Christian, uncouth
strategy of attempting to make people aware of their lost and
sinful condition.'

Quoted by a popular American television pastor

I had a head start when it comes to the knowledge of the fear
and jealousy of God. My old church in Ashland, Kentucky,
was begun in what I would call the 'tail-end' of America's
'second Great Awakening'. The Cane Ridge revival erupted in
Kentucky over a hundred years before and spread all over my
old state and much of the South as well. It began around the

turn of the nineteenth century when people came in their covered wagons to Bourbon Country, Kentucky, for preaching and fellowship. It was the start of the 'camp meeting' phenomenon. One eye-witness wrote:

> People began to fall down . . . This was a new thing among Presbyterians; it excited universal astonishment, and created a curiosity which could not be restrained when people fell during the most solemn parts of divine service . . . [at one point] not less than 1,000 persons fell prostrate to the ground, among whom were many infidels . . . persons falling down were carried out of the crowd, by those next to them, and taken to some convenient place, where prayer is made for them.

Those who fell down were said to be 'totally powerless' just immediately before they fell. Others not so overcome were simply 'unable to stand or sit' but had the 'use of their hands and can converse with perfect composure'. In some cases they were 'unable to speak, the pulse becomes weak, and they draw a difficult breath about once a minute'. For yet others, 'all signs of life forsake them for nearly an hour'. Once they recovered they felt no bodily pain, 'had the entire use of their reason' and could even 'relate everything that had been said or done near them'.

One participant in the Cane Ridge revival told how, having no invitation to preach, he decided to preach anyway by using 'the body of a fallen tree' to stand on. In his own words:

I commenced reading a hymn with an audible voice, and by the time we concluded singing and praying, we had around us, standing on their feet, by fair calculation 10,000 people. I gave out my text . . . 'For we must all stand before the judgment seat of Christ' and before I concluded my voice was not to be heard for the groans of the distressed and the shouts of triumph. Hundreds fell prostrate to the ground, and the work of conversion continued on that spot until Wednesday afternoon. It was estimated by some that not less than 500 were at one time lying on the ground in deepest agonies of distress, and in every few minutes rising in shouts of triumph.

The 'sound of Niagara' was the way the noise was described as their voices could be heard a mile away. This sort of atmosphere swept into many areas of the South and by the early twentieth century was still not uncharacteristic in many churches, including my old church. I was brought up in the Church of the Nazarene and in my town we were nicknamed 'Noisyrenes'. Shouts of praise, however, were paralleled by a great sense of the fear of God in much of the preaching. The man who may be mostly responsible for my early conversion and spiritual development, other than my father, was Dr Gene Phillips. His preaching was absolutely awesome and unforgettable, and engendered such a sense of the fear of God in me that I never outgrew it. This is why I said I had a head start on the subject of this chapter.

The pastor who came to Ashland later on was Dr Harold Daniels. He invited Dr W.M. Tidwell, aged eighty, to hold a series of services that lasted two weeks. On the final Sunday morning Dr Tidwell called me into the pastor's office. I thought I was in trouble! No, he wanted to use me as an illustration (he was a bit eccentric and did this sort of thing). He was going to preach on the parable of the wedding garment and would summon me to come up to him at the appropriate moment in the sermon, to be asked, 'Why do you not have the wedding garment?' I would be 'speechless' and then be bound 'hand and foot' by four of the men in the congregation who were ordered to take me out of the church building – symbolising 'outer darkness' where there would be 'weeping and gnashing of teeth' (Matt. 22:11–13, AV).

I was only about fifteen years old but I remember how people described the effect this illustration had on those assembled. A great sense of the fear of God settled on everybody; that is, everyone except for one girl (whom I knew rather well) who was a year older than I – Patsy. My mother always sat near the front of the church but for some reason was in the back of the auditorium that morning and witnessed Patsy's attitude and behaviour. Patsy laughed and scoffed throughout the entire service, my mother and others said. Many were even worried about her at the time she did this. She snickered as the four men carried me out of the church by the centre aisle, right past where she was seated on the back row, and she continued to show open irreverence.

Old Dr Tidwell gave the 'altar call' and some responded. But he stopped the singing at some point during the invitational hymn to say, 'Someone here this morning is getting their last call. If you do not come to the Lord this morning, you will never again have an opportunity to be saved.' I myself have never said this in a service in my fifty years of preaching and I have never known anybody else to do it. But old Dr Tidwell actually said that. He turned to the pastor, Dr Daniels, and said, 'I will not close this service, I will turn it over to you.' Dr Daniels said he would not close it either and sat down. When Dr Tidwell said that someone was getting their last call, my mother actually wondered if it could be Patsy but did not see how it could possibly refer to someone so young. Slowly people got up to leave, including Patsy, who did not return to the church service that evening.

In those days I was responsible for delivering the local newspaper, the *Ashland Daily Independent*, to about 110 homes each day after I came home from school. When I finished my rounds and returned home, my mother met me on the front porch, crying, 'Have you heard about Patsy?'

'No, what do you mean?'

Sobbing between breaths my mother said, 'She was just killed by a car a few moments ago as she was walking home from school.'

I was sobered from the crown of my head to the soles of my feet. I was gutted as I had never been in my life. What happened was that a car whose driver had not seen the stop sign (some mischievous kids had turned it around) was hit by another car, and it was suddenly shoved onto the sidewalk where Patsy was walking and she was killed instantly. I never went past 25th Street and Montgomery Avenue without remembering that. When I was in Ashland last summer I drove Louise by it to show her the spot.

The effect that moment had on me has never left. It instilled into the utter depths of my soul a sense of the fear of God, the importance of obeying the Holy Spirit and the need to be saved before it is eternally too late. When the Holy Spirit said, 'Today if you will hear his voice, harden not your heart' (Ps. 95:7–8), he really did mean that. People need to be saved or they will be everlastingly lost.

One can sympathise a little bit with the quotation at the beginning of this chapter. Manipulation that is used in evangelism to scare people is not to be condoned. I have seen enough of this too in my old denomination. After all, only the Holy Spirit can make someone see their lost condition. But should the Holy Spirit himself choose to intervene and take over and lead a minister to say what Dr Tidwell said, it could be seen as manipulation; one might call it destructive and counterproductive. But when one recalls the atmosphere of the fear of God on the people and the horrible thing that happened the following day, I conclude it was not a manipulative ploy at all; it was God graciously warning people. But it wasn't very nice.

Our Pilot Light ministry in London (ministering on the streets near Buckingham Gate and Victoria) continued non-stop (save for Christmas and Boxing Day) for the last twenty years I was at Westminster Chapel. We have presented the gospel to thousands. Hundreds made professions. Were they all saved? I know some of them were and suspect a lot more were converted (at the time or eventually) than we realised. During my last days there where I always witnessed (on the steps in front of the Chapel) I gave a tract translated into German to a young man. A few months later, after our retirement, a letter came from him in Germany to our present home in Key Largo, Florida. He said he had been praying for his father for years and years with no apparent success. But he gave my tract to his dad. He wrote to say his father received Christ as his Lord and Saviour when he read the tract – and suddenly died the next day. I used to urge Pilot Lights to present the gospel 'as though their destiny were in their hands and yours because they may never hear the gospel again'.

We live in what Dr O.S. Hawkins calls 'the No Fear culture'. O.S. suggests it is because 'our generation knows little of the nature of God'. People in and out of the Church have no fear of God. He defines the fear of God as being 'a reverential awe, a sense of being afraid of offending a holy God in any way'. I am glad he is not afraid to use the word 'afraid'. So many water down the fear of God by quickly saying, 'Now it doesn't mean to be afraid of God.' Really? It certainly does mean that; otherwise nobody will begin to feel real respect and awe for the God of the Bible. I have no doubt that at times when the Bible refers to people walking in the fear of the Lord in fact they were scared to death.

The fear of God is a no-nonsense and a no-joke thing. It is very real when described in the Bible and is often intended to strike fear in us. It should shake us to our fingertips. It did in the early Church. This is what generally characterised the atmosphere when Jesus performed miracles and when the apostles preached the gospel. Many modern versions translate the Greek word *phobos* as 'awe' – which of course it is. But I sometimes think 'awe' does not always mediate the feeling the writers intended when they used the *phobos* (from which we get the suffix 'phobia'). For example, the first time the word 'fear' appears in the New Testament was when the angel said to Joseph, 'Fear not to take unto thee Mary thy wife' (Matt. 1:20, AV). Clearly the writer did not mean, 'Do not be in awe'. The

NIV rightly translates this phrase, 'Do not be afraid . . .', and yet not using the word 'fear' in so many instances could somehow make many miss the actual feeling the writer wanted to convey. This is partly because the word 'awe' can also mean admiration, and the word 'awesome' today can mean even 'neat' or 'cool'.

I doubt not that when Jesus healed the paralysed man who was presented to Jesus through the roof they glorified God and 'were filled with fear' (Luke 5:26, AV). When a boy was raised from the dead, 'there came fear on all' (Luke 7:16, AV). When the residents in the country of the Gerasenes urged Jesus to leave the area because the demon-possessed man had been miraculously delivered it was because 'they were taken with great fear' (Luke 8:37, AV).

This theme continues in the book of Acts. One forgotten fall-out of the happenings on the day of Pentecost was that 'fear came upon every soul' (Acts 2:43, AV). When Ananias was struck dead for lying to the Holy Spirit, 'great fear came on all' (Acts 5:5, AV), as was the case shortly after that when, after the same thing happened to Sapphira, 'great fear came upon all the church' (Acts 5:11, AV). Later on, when Saul of Tarsus was converted, the church had an era of rest and peace and yet they were still found 'walking in the fear of the Lord' (Acts 9:31, AV). When the sons of Sceva failed in their attempt to cast out demons but were overcome by them, the result was that 'fear fell on them all, and the name of the Lord Jesus was magnified' (Acts 19:17, AV). Paul said, 'Them that sin rebuke before all, that others also may fear' (1 Tim. 5:20, AV). Noah 'moved with fear' in his obedience to God (Heb. 11:7, AV). The effect of the lightning and thunder at Mount Sinai for Moses was, 'I exceedingly fear and quake' (Heb. 12:21, AV). We are commanded to serve God with 'reverence and godly fear' (Heb. 12:28, AV). Peter admonished us to 'pass the time of your sojourning here in fear' (1 Pet. 1:17, AV).

This is to take absolutely nothing from the fact that the earliest Church equally and simultaneously experienced great joy. The same disciples who were filled with fear were equally 'filled with joy' (Acts 13:52). When people saw the miraculous in Samaria there was 'great joy' there (Acts 8:8). Similarly, the news of Gentiles being converted resulted in 'great joy' (Acts 15:3, AV). And in case you think it is impossible to have joy and fear simultaneously, I would remind you that when Jesus was raised from the dead the women who heard the report from the angels were both 'afraid yet filled with joy' (Matt. 28:8).

The first message of the New Testament was to 'flee from the coming wrath' (Matt. 3:7). Why would a person flee – which means 'run'? Because to grasp the meaning of John the Baptist's message meant they were to be afraid of the coming wrath. Not just politely to tip the hat toward God or show a bit of respectful deference but to be truly in fear of what was coming. It is my view that the revival that is coming will usher in simultaneous fear and joy to the people. It will send terror to the lost and to the backslidden and bring both fear and joy to those found walking in the light.

What does walking in the fear of the Lord mean? It certainly does mean to worship with reverence and awe. But it means to live in fear of displeasing the Lord. I realise that there are always those (and every pastor faces this) who are overly conscientious – almost to the point of being neurotic – when this kind of teaching is carried out. And I certainly would not want to add to anyone's anxiety unnecessarily in these lines.

But let me explain what I mean. A deep and true fear of God will keep you from committing adultery – because of what it does to God, to the Church, to the one you would be involved with, to your spouse and family, and to you. A fear of God will mean that we are afraid to kill anybody for the same reasons. But when we develop a sensitivity to the Holy Spirit, we are equally afraid to commit adultery in our *heart*, to hurt another person's *reputation*, to hold a *grudge* or to do anything to bring vengeance. The Sermon on the Mount was given to develop a true fear of the Lord, shown by the way we live.

The Holy Spirit mirrors the God of the Bible and is as sensitive to what displeases the Father as the Father himself. Therefore when we develop a care not to grieve the Holy Spirit we will do nothing knowingly that would bring him displeasure. It is a healthy Christian who fears God's chastening, or his disciplining us. Said the psalmist, 'O LORD, do not rebuke me in your anger or discipline me in your wrath' (Ps. 6:1, 'hot displeasure', AV). The reason God disciplines us is because of his jealous love.

The verse that I have sought to have govern me more than any other is John 5:44. I was initially influenced by the Authorised Version: 'How can ye believe, which receive honour one of another, and seek not the honour that cometh from God only?' This translation stresses the honour that only God – not people – is prepared to bestow, that we should seek his pleasure and approval alone. Most versions translate 'the only God', which does not change the aforementioned meaning. But if there is a blessing that comes from seeking only his approval and not the affirmation of each other, I for one want this.

John 5:44 assumes that God is jealous. He doesn't like it when we opt for human approval rather than his alone. This is exactly what the ancient Jews did and the precise reason they missed their own Messiah when he came. When Jesus stood before the Jews and they rejected him he told them why they were blind: it is because they seek honour from one another and that they did not seek the honour that comes from the only true God. Had they been seeking his honour instead of each other's they would have recognised the One God sent to them. Hence Jesus asked, 'How can you believe [in other words, 'You are not able to believe'] when you do not make any real attempt to receive the honour that comes from God alone?'

In a word: when we seek his honour over the approval of people, God rewards us – whether with vindication, other good things or with insight; when we seek the approval of people instead, God's jealousy sets in and he withholds such blessings, including insight. That is what happened to ancient Israel in Jesus' day. They knew that he was a jealous God. But they let pride rule – wanting approval of each other, not what God wanted to give them.

This principle still applies. John 5:44 is one of those verses that grips me to such depths that I am often overcome with godly fear. I have wanted to write a book on this verse more than anything else in the world. I think the only reason I have not written a book on this is that God won't show me more about this verse than I need to know. It could be that my own desire to write such a book is of the flesh and an unconscious desire to get the applause of people for writing such a book –

and God himself withholds further insight I need. I only know that he won't bend the rules for any of us. And while my desire might be a godly one to some extent, chances are that my real motive is for my receiving honour from people. All I know is, I am not able so far to write such a book – and I certainly know too little about God's glory. It is perhaps what happened when Moses walked up to the burning bush (to see why it didn't burn up) and God told him to stop! 'Do not come any closer . . . take off your sandals . . . you are standing [on] holy ground' (Exod. 3:5). God won't explain everything we are curious about; he just says, 'Stop! Take off your shoes.'

I know this much: the fear of God is what we must demonstrate in our hearts and by our lives as well as to respect his jealousy, and it is required of each of us. He wants all the glory for everything. Like it or not, that is the way he is. When he makes a covenant with his people he expects them to honour it. Israel didn't and they missed the very One they were so sure they would recognise and accept when he came. God rolled up his sleeves and inflicted blindness on Israel's best scholars and leaders. Relatively few Jews got in on the blessing.

Jonathan Edwards taught us that the task of every generation is to discover in which direction the Sovereign Redeemer is moving, then move in that direction. I can think of nothing worse than to miss seeing and participating in what God is in fact the instigator of. If I am seeking his honour with all my heart I am assured I will not miss what he is doing in our day. When he is at work and people say, 'That's not God', it is blindness in operation and almost certainly traceable to the fear of others and the pride in us that makes us want people's approval most of all. But he is a jealous God – always has been, always will be. Get used to it. That is the way he is. Jealous.

There are therefore certain qualities among God's attributes, or characteristics, that are not regarded as very flattering when applied to people. Take, for example, the sensitivity of the Holy Spirit, which we have mentioned before. It is hardly possible to exaggerate how sensitive the Holy Spirit is, how easily he gets his feelings hurt. When Paul said, 'Do not grieve the Holy Spirit of God, with whom you were sealed for the day of redemption' (Eph. 4:30), he used a word – *lupeite* (Greek translated 'grieve') – that means 'to get one's feelings hurt'. When we speak of a person who is highly sensitive to criticism – who gets their feelings hurt easily – it is not a compliment. 'Be careful around that person – you must walk on eggshells around them.' Not a nice thing to have said about you.

One of the most surprising aspects of God's personality, then, is that he is jealous by nature. He is very 'up front' about it. He even says that his very name is Jealous! 'Do not worship any other god, for the LORD, whose name is Jealous, is a jealous God' (Exod. 34:14). Not a very flattering thing to have said about us. I don't want to admit it when I am jealous. I don't want to be that vulnerable before you. But he admits it.

Jealousy is one of those traits about frail human beings that we can easily see in another person but we are often the last to see in ourselves. We dare not admit to such insecurity. We dare not admit that a particular person 'gets our goat'. It is embarrassing to admit that the way we feel about a person – as often the real reason we do not like them – is because we are jealous. We would not want that person we dislike to be so flattered!

Strange as it may seem, the jealousy that is seen as a product of our sinful nature (see Gal. 5:19–21) is the very word used to describe the God of the Bible. He can be like that. But we can't! But is this unfair? I can only reply with the words God spoke through the prophet:

'For my thoughts are not your thoughts, neither are your ways my ways,' declares the LORD. 'As the heavens are higher than the earth, so are my ways higher than your ways and my thoughts than your thoughts.' (Isa. 55:8–9)

To put it plainly, when God does not get his way he becomes angry. He may not show it at first. Sometimes *the angrier he is the longer he waits* to bring vengeance. But when he does not have his way with us – his covenant people – his jealousy kicks in and it is only a matter of time before it is openly manifested. He does not appear to be very nice when he does not get his way.

It is this very thing that often, perhaps more than anything else, puts people off the God of the Bible.

I will never forget how this struck me when I was at seminary in Louisville, Kentucky. In a preaching class each of us had the task of preaching for twenty minutes to the other students in the class. When my turn came I chose Romans 8:28 for my text: 'And we know that all things work together for good to them that love God, to them who are the called according to his purpose' (AV). I expounded it the way I continue to do – that whatever happens to us (good or bad or even our sin) will eventually work together for good if we love God and are 'the called according to his purpose'.

The students, at least many of them, reacted very negatively. They replied that my sermon was 'All God, God, God' and 'All about his glory and nothing about us'. Inwardly I was chuffed that my sermon came through like that – I could not have received a higher compliment. But they hoped it would defeat me and humble me. But the episode was a kind of revelation to me; these students and I were operating in entirely different wavelengths. The very things they hated most about God – his glory and honour – were the very things that thrilled me most. One student, though no happier than the others, came to my defence somewhat and admitted, 'After all, what R.T. has said about Romans 8:28 is what Paul really said – I just don't agree with Paul!' In other words, he didn't like the truth of Romans 8:28.

Romans 8:28 shows God's jealous love for his own, how God is determined that whatever affects us affects him as well and therefore he is determined to make sure all that happens to us, sooner or later, works together for good. Because his honour is at stake. It is a gracious fringe benefit of the truth of God's jealousy.

This is what happened when Ananias and Sapphira lied to the Holy Spirit (Acts 5:1–11). I doubt this couple were the first to lie to God, neither were they the last. But at that time God chose to show his jealousy and strike them dead – a clear manifestation of his glory. He was jealous for his glory in the Church. There was a very high level of his manifest presence in the Church in those days. It was a foolish and dangerous thing to play fast and loose with his glory at such a time as that. I have long believed this is why Ananias and Sapphira did not get away with what they did at a time when God was doing wonderful things among his people. When God's power is being displayed, one would be better off to play with a million volts of electricity with wet hands than to play games with the Holy Spirit.

Consider what was going on in the book of Acts. A prayer meeting when the place was shaken – possibly a small earthquake (Acts 4:31) – had resulted in great power and witness by the Holy Spirit to the people regarding Jesus' resurrection. So powerful was the Spirit's presence that the resurrection of Jesus was as real to them as if they had seen it with their very eyes. This is how powerfully God can turn up with his people – to make clear the truths of redemption as though we were eye-witnesses. And when that kind of power is around we should take off our shoes and worship. A further result at the time was that the people became utterly detached from material things. Some might say that they lost their heads. And maybe they did. Whatever, they voluntarily sold their properties and laid the proceeds of the sales at the apostles' feet. As far as I know, we are not commanded to do this in any verse in the Bible. But it is what they chose to do.

Nobody was required to do what many were doing, including Ananias and Sapphira. Therefore Ananias and Sapphira could have opted out and said to the rest, 'You can do this if you want, but we don't think we will do this.' Had they said that there would have been no problem. Their fatal mistake was that they wanted to appear to be in on what was happening and pretended to lay all their proceeds at the apostles' feet – but in fact kept part of the money for themselves. This too might have been all right had they said, 'We are only giving part of the money.' But no. They pretended to give all as others had done. The high level of power and great measure of God's presence meant that the apostles discerned their mockery. God killed them.

I sometimes think of foolish things I have done in my lifetime – much worse (I would have thought) than what Ananias and Sapphira did. But God didn't kill me. He could have. Perhaps he should have. And yet I think he would have, had there been a manifestation of his power and glory at the time. The absence of that glory was possibly what saved me from being taken home abruptly to heaven like Ananias and Sapphira were. (Yes, I believe they were saved.)

Perhaps I should say I am glad that God was not in the process of showing his glory at times in my life which, if I make myself think about them, make me blush – and scared. Why should God be so gracious to me? Why should he not give me the treatment he gave to Ananias and Sapphira?

I know only this: 'The whole earth is full of his glory' (Isa. 6:3). This means that God could, if he wanted, call any of us at any moment to give an account of our thoughts and actions.

When Arthur Blessitt first came to Westminster Chapel in 1982, he shook us rigid. Upstanding and well-respected people were leaving the church. One deacon – whom I loved – said to me during the time of Arthur's visit, 'The trouble is, do we really want revival?', candidly implying he wasn't so sure he wanted it after all! He could see the cost – the price you pay: overcoming pride, fear and tradition. True revival is so disruptive. Things were starting to happen in those days. It got messy.

I always hoped for true and full-blown revival to come to Westminster Chapel while I was there. It never did – certainly not in the measure I longed for. I believe it will come. But had it come in the great measure I dreamed of, it might have meant a recurrence of people being found out and moved on like Ananias and Sapphira were.

Have you ever wondered why certain people in Corinth were either weak, sick or died – all because they abused the Lord's Supper? God's glory was at stake; his jealousy was aroused. The poor people of Corinth (slaves who had to work late) were being stepped on and walked over by the more affluent and smug believers who did not wait for the poor to arrive for communion. Paul had to tell them why some of them were weak or ill or had died. And yet those who were so disciplined by the Lord were truly converted, saved people. Paul said they were 'judged by the Lord' in order that they not be condemned with the world; which would mean eternal punishment, not the chastening these had experienced (1 Cor. 11:17–34).

In a word: I have been guilty of some of the same things that characterised people who were severely judged by the Holy Spirit. I know I have been smug and arrogant and did not care one whit for the poor at earlier times in my life. I am so ashamed. What saved me was possibly the absence of the manifestation of the presence of God. I would hope I am in better shape now. But many don't want revival because smugness is one of the first things to be judged.

The revival that is needed (and which I happen to believe is coming) is the *Eschaton* (the Last Day) being brought forward to the here and now – at least for a while. It is when there is a clear sense of God – of joy and mourning, mercy and judgment – just as it will be when we all stand before the judgment seat of Christ (2 Cor. 5:10). On that day every deed will be exposed – then judged or rewarded. I therefore thank God, I am ashamed to say it, that revival did not come at certain times in my life when my heart was cold – full of doubt, cynicism and unbelief. But God was merciful to me, that's about all I can say. I would have to admit, moreover, that he was, surely, nice to me until I was brought to a place of repentance.

But knowing as I do now something of the fear of the Lord, I have sought to live my life in a manner that, were God to show up, I would be ready. Being ready for revival is like being ready for the Second Coming. It comes suddenly.

'Between the times' (a phrase I learned from Richard Bewes) is when God largely does not show his jealousy. He remains jealous – watching over us in whole detail. We should therefore live each day as if God would manifest his presence in great measure – and such a time be great joy for us rather than grief.

For the Lord does not change (Mal. 3:6). His name is still Jealous. Were this truth to grip us as it should, it would literally change our thinking, our lives and our attitude.

God is jealous because he loves us so much. It is truly wonderful that he is a jealous God. He wants only what is best for us. For this reason, his jealousy flares up when we show deference to other gods – the world, the flesh and the devil. When we become more enamoured with approval and honour from his people than the honour that comes only from him, he doesn't like it one bit.

The purpose of this chapter and this book is to change the life of the person who reads it – you. When we see his displeasure and how he can show his anger, it ought to have at least a twofold effect: first, to thank him for his patience with us and second, to be different from now on and live under the gracious fear of God.

It is an irony that the very thing God does to get our attention is often the very thing that puts us off him: the hiding of his face, the unanswered prayer, the way he chooses to be absent when he is (apparently) needed most. But this very thing is actually his way of leading us to repentance. The goodness of God leads us to repentance (Rom. 2:4, AV) but that goodness appears at first to be the opposite of that – like striking people dead. Or manifesting his power in a manner that is utterly off-putting to us who are sophisticated.

I said above that I believe that the revival that is needed is on the way. Get ready for it. It will be a mirroring of the true God and will show what really is in the hearts of men and women. People generally will not be happy with the God who will be manifested. At least not at first. But many will be converted. It will be the manifestation of the God of the Bible most people are not prepared for. But neither will it be our projection upon the backdrop of the universe. For no human being could come up with the God who will shortly be revealed. But if that revival is for some reason delayed, you will still come face to face with him. For there is one inevitable fact – we are all going to die and 'after that to face judgment' (Heb. 9:27). Therefore whether it is revival that is on the way – or death – we will meet the true God.

You will certainly be out of your comfort zone then. But there is an exception to this. John talked about being 'unashamed' before him (1 John 2:28), even having 'confidence' on the day of judgment (1 John 4:17). That is an amazing possibility. It is the consequence of walking in the light – that uncreated light of the true God in whom there is no darkness (1 John 1:5,7). The result is that the blood of Jesus cleanses us from all sin. That is how the amazing possibility of being bold before him – whether at his second coming, death or during the revival I envisage – comes about. It is seeing who the real God is. And loving him for being as he is. Will you love him for being as he is? What follows in the chapters below is an attempt to describe him little by little, like peeling the layers of an onion. But it is only an attempt. We will never see him as he fully is until he unveils himself in his ultimate glory at his Son's coming. And even then we will just begin to learn more about him.

What if there really is a hell?

I close this chapter with the above question not because I am questioning whether there is a hell but in the light of both massive repudiation of the historic teaching of eternal punishment by many stalwart scholars of the New Testament; and also the strange neglect of preaching on this subject by those who claim they do believe in hell. I would define hell as God's idea to create a place of unending conscious punishment of those who loved darkness rather than light and would not come to the light. Jesus said,

> This is the verdict: Light has come into the world, but men loved darkness instead of light because their deeds were evil. Everyone who does evil hates the light, and will not come into the light for fear that his deeds will be exposed. (John 3:19–20)

I think I have given more thought and prayer to this subject than any in this book or, for that matter, any in the Bible. Along with me, I presume, the doctrine of eternal punishment of the lost does not seem right or fair to you. If I could press a button and make one of two things happen in one stroke it would be:

1   that the purported doctrine of annihilation is true after all; or

2   universalism is true – the idea that everybody will be saved and nobody lost.

I do not believe the Bible teaches either but I would be glad if it did – or if it were discovered after we get to heaven that there was some 'loophole' or clear teaching right there before our eyes in Holy Scripture that we couldn't see before. I know people who think it is clear now – and make a case for annihilation. Not many who call themselves Evangelicals would make a case for universalism; this has been the teaching of certain non-Evangelicals who do not hold to the infallibility of Holy Scripture as I do. Annihilation is the teaching that the lost will be annihilated – utterly destroyed – so that there are no remains of the person in any way – body, memory, soul or spirit. Annihilation renders them as non-existent, as though they were not created in the first place.

You will recall my referring to Ludwig Feuerbach at the beginning of this book. He claimed that God is nothing more than man's projection upon the backdrop of the universe. God does not exist, said Feuerbach; he exists only in our minds; we project a God who is 'out there' who will look after us – and take us to heaven when we die.

Given that premiss, I ask: whoever would have projected the doctrine of hell on the backdrop of the universe? What rational, normal and humane person would conceive of the teaching of hell? To me this is an appropriate question to put to the followers of Feuerbach. It disproves his theory – unless there is no hell – for no sensible human being would have come up with this teaching. This is not a God who only takes care of us or receives us in heaven but a God who is angry and punishes in a manner no person would have conceived or wanted to believe.

But could it be true? Is it conceivable that the New Testament really does teach us that people go to either heaven or hell when they die and that both places are inhabited by conscious people with memories and feelings and that both states never come to an end? Heaven is never-ending bliss – occupied by those who received Jesus Christ as Lord and Saviour; hell is unending punishment – occupied by those who did not receive Jesus Christ as Lord and Saviour.

Some of us might be tempted to say that the Bible was written by people in a pre-scientific age and that such a teaching was plausible and accepted then. But now that people have 'come of age', to quote Dietrich Bonhoeffer (1906–1945), such a teaching is surely out of the question, not a few would say. Moreover, a loving God would not expect us to believe in such a horrible doctrine.

It has been somewhat surprising that good and capable scholars of the New Testament have 'come out of hiding' in recent years to say that they do not believe in conscious eternal punishment for the wicked, and to claim that the Bible doesn't teach it either. There is some impressive evidence for their point of view, by the way. A lot of sincere Christians get indignant that such preachers exist ('How could they call themselves Christians?' some ask), but these ministers, it is only fair to say, do not reject eternal punishment merely because they don't want to believe it; they point to what they feel is the biblical evidence for the teaching of the annihilation of the wicked.

An entire book to treat the issue is called for; this section is but a drop in the bucket as to what is needed. I would recommend Wayne Grudem, *Systematic Theology* (Inter-Varsity Press, 1994). I myself have treated the subject briefly in *Understanding Theology* (Christian Focus, 1996). I follow a principle that I do not write a book when another person has ably and responsibly written one on the same subject, nor would I repeat much of what I myself have written elsewhere. However, I will mention briefly two things some of my friends (whom I love and respect) want to say in support of the teaching of annihilation. The first is that the Greek word *apollumi* means 'to perish' or 'to destroy' and that Jesus said that those who believe in him 'shall not perish' (*apollumi*, John 3:16). Thus those who do not believe, then, simply perish: they are annihilated. I will respond to this below.

The second thing that those who teach annihilation tell us is that the traditional view of eternal punishment is largely based upon the Greek idea of the 'immortality of the soul'. Many of us have taken for granted that the soul of the person, given to them by creation, is immortal; the soul lives on even though the body dies. This is based partly on the fact that we are made in the image of God (Gen. 1:26–27). He alone has immortality in himself (1 Tim. 6:16) – yes, but he chose to bestow this on all the human race through creation. But we are now being told that this is only a Greek idea, not Hebraic, and that the Bible never taught the immortality of the soul in the first place. This makes it easier to accept the teaching of annihilation – a position taken by the cults over the years, including Jehovah's Witnesses, but which is now being embraced by a growing number of Evangelicals.

According to this point of view, which is spreading like wildfire on both sides of the Atlantic, the soul is not given immortality until the person is born again. The traditional view (which happens to be my own) has been that the person is given immortality by creation – by being *born*. So if a person is given immortality of the soul when they are born, that person's soul survives death; but if the person is not given immortality of the soul until they are *born again*, only the *Christian's* soul lives beyond the grave. The person who is not a Christian therefore does not have an immortal soul (according to this view); the person dies – that's it; no immortal soul even to be annihilated. The person simply ceases to exist.

Some, however, teach that the unsaved will be raised to face judgment, and will be annihilated after that. But the point is this: if the soul of the unsaved is not immortal, there is no hell awaiting the unregenerate; only the painless, instantaneous annihilation of the person by the fires of hell. These people want to emphasise that they do not deny hell; they deny only that hell is conscious, never-ending punishment. Hell to them means annihilation.

Regarding the Greek word *apollumi*, which is translated 'perish' in John 3:16, there is no use of the word in the New Testament that clearly indicates annihilation. You can interpret it that way if you choose to in some places, but one would not be likely to think of annihilation if they were not looking for it and wanting that meaning. If the New Testament writers wanted to make it clear that they meant annihilation they should have used the Greek word *ekmedenisis* (which clearly means 'annihilation') or *ekmedenizo* (to annihilate) – words that were in currency then. Furthermore, there are times when *apollumi* (or the noun form) could not mean 'annihilation'. For example, when some complained about the expensive perfume that was being poured on Jesus, they asked, 'Why this *waste*?' (*apoleia*, the noun form of *apollumi*). The perfume was wasted, they said. That is hardly annihilation. A modern equivalent is when an insurance company regards a wrecked car as a 'write-off'. It is now waste. And, I have to say it with all love and honesty, that is what happens to the person who blows away the privilege that was theirs by not coming to the light. They will sadly be an everlasting waste. Forever. That is the meaning of the Greek word *apollumi* or *apoleia* when it is translated 'destruction' or 'perishing'.

The question I often put to people who know neither Greek nor ancient philosophy is this: if you merely read the teachings of Jesus without any bias whatever, what would you suppose *he* was teaching (even if you disagree with him)? And what do you really think his *hearers* perceived (even if they were ignorant and simple people)? Take the parable, or story, in Luke 16:19–31 as related by Jesus. Two people died. One of them (named Lazarus) went to Abraham's side, the other (who was called a 'rich man') was found in hell. 'In hell [Greek, *hades*] where he was in torment, he looked up and saw Abraham far away, with Lazarus by his side' (Luke 16:23). Since the physical bodies of

Lazarus and the rich man were still in the grave, one assumes it was the souls, or the spirits, of Abraham and the rich man that are described. Whatever you want to call them, both men were very conscious after death; one was with Abraham (who apparently had been in that heavenly realm for hundreds of years), the other in torment.

In my book the *Parables of Jesus* (Sovereign World, 2003), I state that you cannot make a parable stand 'on all four legs' – which means you can't make a doctrine out of every point in a parable that is basically teaching one truth. But in this account, even if eternal punishment *wasn't* the main point (although I believe it was), Jesus would hardly have given throwaway comments about a matter so awful if the truth about conscious punishment after death was not an assumption in his thinking or inconceivable by his hearers. If the account of the rich man and Lazarus was revealing new truth, what he said must be taken seriously. If this account only assumed these things, we need to see why they were mentioned. As for the immortality of the soul being a gift of the Spirit at conversion and not creation, how does one explain the rich man – obviously unconverted – who was in conscious torment in *hades* – which means either a place of punishment or the grave? It wasn't his *physical body* in hell so it had to be his soul or spirit, which survived the grave. What is obvious is that the man was in conscious torment. Jesus also indicated that the two states are permanent and unchangeable, both at Abraham's side – which I take to be a metaphor for Paradise or heaven – or in *hades*, which means 'hell' in this parable.

What became known as 'the New Testament teaching on hell' is based upon various descriptions which seem to be referring to the same thing: outer darkness, eternal punishment, weeping and gnashing of teeth, a furnace of fire, damnation and other things. As to whether the fire is literal, I certainly hope it is not and would make a case that it need not be literal. I would point to the real possibility that references to torment by fire are metaphors and are not literal. For example, if Jesus could refer to eating his flesh and blood (when he meant Holy Communion), or to raising up the temple in three days (when he meant not the temple in Jerusalem but the resurrection of his body), or to the yeast of the Pharisees (meaning their teaching), then he could well have meant something other than literal fire when referring to hell. This is what I hope is true. It hopefully refers to the pain of the soul that is unbearable in the light of missing heaven – which could have been one's eternal state. That is horrible enough in any case.

I do not try to prove that hell exists in this chapter. Jesus did not try to prove that it existed – he only assumed it when he preached. He also taught that the only evidence for its existence is to be found in the Bible. The rich man in hell pleaded that Lazarus be raised from the dead to convince his brothers who did not believe hell existed. Jesus replied that they should believe the Word of God – the only basis for believing it (Luke 16:30–31).

I believe hell exists. It was entirely God's idea. 'Shall not the Judge of all the earth do right?' (Gen. 18:25). When John the Baptist warned people to 'flee from the coming wrath' (Matt. 3:7) – arguably the first message of the New Testament, and eternal punishment was exactly what he meant – his warning made sense. I doubt people would *run* from coming wrath with much concern if they knew in advance it meant only annihilation. Annihilation becomes the same kind of non-existence the unbeliever is counting on when they die. What perhaps worries me most about the promotion of the idea of annihilation is that it hands on a silver platter a *theological* rationale to unbelievers – precisely what they were hoping in the first place was true. They say, 'Why should I believe? Why should I give up my way of life? I will eventually end up as though I never lived – no unending hell to fear.'

The teaching of Jesus regarding hell was not meant to make us comfortable. He had more to say about hell than he did about heaven. People sometimes say, 'I believe in heaven but I don't believe in hell.' I answer: if there is no hell, there is no heaven. The two rise or fall together. As for Jesus' teaching on hell, it blasts us out of our comfort zone. For the God who conceived of the teaching of hell and who created hell is not very nice. It's not my idea, I can assure you. No human being would have thought this up.

But what if it is true? It makes all the difference in our outlook, our evangelism, our view of God and our sense of gratitude that we ourselves will not spend eternity in hell. I think of William Booth's address to the first graduation class of the Salvation Army. He said that he felt like apologising to them for keeping them for two years to learn how to lead a soul to Christ. 'It would be better had you spent five minutes in hell', he said, because that way they could be effective soul winners on their own. I thank God we don't have to spend any time there.

My old friend Rolfe Barnard used to say, 'Ladies and gentlemen, the blood of Jesus and the fires of hell go together.' Why? There are two ways by which God ultimately punishes sin: either by the sacrifice of his Son, whose blood *completely and eternally* satisfies his justice; or the fires of hell, which never completely satisfies his justice – which is why hell is unending.

Is your God too nice? Is your God One who would not punish? Is he One who lets you rest comfortably in your sphere of existence without any worries about the lost – or the state of the Church being so irrelevant? Or the state of your own soul? Does he let you stay indefinitely in your comfort zone? I am talking about the God of the Bible.

4

The Sovereignty of God

'But Mr Spurgeon, what if we convert one of the non-elect?'
'Don't worry, my boy', replied the great Charles Haddon
Spurgeon, 'God will forgive you for that.'

I did not always believe what I will teach in this chapter. I was
not brought up to believe in what follows, not even remotely.
The people I knew back in Kentucky who believed some of
what I shall elaborate on in this chapter went to such extremes
with it that it was enough to put most reasonable and thinking
people right off the subject. It is hard to say which is more
true: that it is the most abused teaching in church history or
that, rightly understood, it is the most needed in the Church at
the present time. Because the latter I believe is true I shall do
my best to introduce it, as though you knew little or nothing
of it, and yet show why it is definitely needed.

My discovery of the truth of the sovereignty of God came

as a result of my 'Damascus Road' experience on 31 October 1955. When I refer to it in that manner, however, I do not mean my conversion, as it was in the case of Saul of Tarsus, but to a work of the Holy Spirit many years after I was saved, which I now believe was the baptism of the Holy Spirit. It led to an enormous change in my life but also my theology – not in the essentials of the faith but in very important truths of the Bible none the less.

It not only made the Bible become alive in my heart more powerfully than I had ever known but also led me to teachings in the Bible I did not know were there! I no longer read the Bible defensively or with the aim of proving a certain point of view. I just wanted to know what the Bible was saying and was prepared to believe it – no matter where it led.

This happened to me when I was a student at Trevecca Nazarene College of Nashville, Tennessee. I was also pastor of a small country church on a mountain in Palmer, Tennessee. On the way back to Trevecca one Monday morning, the glory of the Lord filled the car – and there was the Lord Jesus himself interceding for me at the right hand of God. It was as real as if it were physical or tangible. I entered into a rest of soul – I experienced a peace that I did not know was possible in this life. The Lord Jesus was more real to me than anything around me. If nothing more than that happened, it was still the greatest experience of my life.

But more followed before the day was over. Waves of glory swept over me and it was renewed. I was given an infallible assurance of my salvation – I knew I was eternally saved, and with that an awareness that what had happened to me was a work of the Holy Spirit. I now know it as a sovereign work. It was what God *alone* did. I knew I could not make it happen, neither could I make this happen for anybody else. From this came a focus on certain Scriptures in the New Testament that meant – here comes the controversial part – election or predestination. Such had been utterly alien to me but now very, very real to me. I knew there was truth to this teaching despite the fact that my old church taught against it. Some even said the teaching was of the devil and 'born in hell'. All I knew was, it was true – despite what I had been taught as I grew up.

This drove me to the Word of God. At first I thought I was the first to have this understanding since the apostle Paul! I thought that what had happened to me was unprecedented. I was wrong. Not only was it not new; I had tapped into the theological mainstream of the Christian Church. I was amazed to discover this and I have never got over it. Why me? Why would God show this to me? Better still, why did God save me? What had I done to deserve to be saved? If one said, 'But you followed your parents' teaching and received the Lord because you wanted to please your parents', I would say, 'If that is true, why did I want to do this? Others have had Christian parents but rebelled. Why should I want to receive Jesus?'

I knew the answer was that God was being exceedingly gracious to me. I could take no credit for anything. I began to see things in the Bible for myself which made me know God was powerfully with me. What startled me most of all perhaps was that so many of the great men in history believed this – hundreds of years ago. John Newton, author of 'Amazing grace', for example. In my church the hymn 'Amazing grace' was sung almost every week. When I found out that John Newton believed these things the Holy Spirit had shown me it was such an encouragement. I discovered too that the Pilgrim Fathers who settled in America believed this teaching. What thrilled me more was to discover that this teaching was central to the theology of one of my heroes – Jonathan Edwards, the leading preacher in the Great Awakening of the eighteenth century.

I have to say that it did not greatly bless my father or my grandmother. They were appalled that I had embraced a teaching that they felt was contrary to the way the Lord had led them. Indeed my grandmother had come from the very theological background (which she had turned against) that I was now upholding. Those were hard days.

I don't want to imply that if you don't agree with what I will expound below it means you are not a good Christian or that you are not following the Lord with all your heart. Neither would I want to say that someone has not experienced the baptism of the Spirit if it did not lead them to the same truths I have come to embrace. As a matter of fact, I have run into countless people who have indeed received the baptism of the Spirit and not one of them, as far as I know, was led in the same theological direction as me. So I am not saying for one moment that there is something wrong with you if you don't agree with me. Not at all. I simply do not understand why I have been led the way I have.

My mentor and professor at Trevecca, Dr William Greathouse (who has remained a close friend over the years), said to me in astonishment in those days, 'R.T., you are going off into Calvinism.'

I said, 'What is that?'

He replied, 'We don't believe that in our church.'

I retorted, 'Then we are wrong.' I asked him, referring to Romans 9:14–23, to explain what was meant. He said he needed more time on that – and this was some fifty years ago. 'R.T., don't leave our church', he pleaded. At that stage I had no plans to leave. But it was inevitable. All who knew me in those days were absolutely convinced that I would change my mind in time. My old church followed John Wesley, and he still is greatly admired by me, but he certainly spoke against many of the things that I will put forward in this chapter. He stood adamantly against the theology of George Whitefield, who espoused what I believe, and both of these men are in heaven today.

The sovereignty of God is what lay behind the betrayal of Jesus and his being crucified. It was no accident. Things did not go wrong. Jesus forecast his crucifixion.

'The Son of Man is going to be betrayed into the hands of men. They will kill him, and on the third day he will be raised to life' (Matt. 17:22–23). ' "My food," said Jesus, "is to do the will of him who sent me and to finish his work" ' (John 4:34). As he further predicted his death Jesus said, 'Now my heart is troubled, and what shall I say? "Father, save me from this hour"? No, it was for this very reason I came to this hour. Father, glorify your name!' (John 12:27–28). Among Jesus' last words were these: 'It is finished' (John 19:30), a translation of *tetelestai* which was a colloquial expression in the ancient market place that meant 'paid in full'. Jesus' death on the cross was more than a crucifixion; it was atonement.

Indeed, it was what God did. 'The LORD has laid on him the iniquity of us all . . . It was the LORD's will to crush him and cause him to suffer' (Isa. 53:6,10). For this reason, when Peter preached the inaugural sermon of the Church on the day of Pentecost, he declared: 'This man was handed over to you by God's set *purpose and foreknowledge;* and you, with the help of wicked men, put him to death by nailing him to the cross' (Acts 2:23). This shows that the same God who predestined the end also predestined the means to the end. This is a consistent principle in the sovereignty of God and man's role in all he does. Always. The two work together and cohere. The end in this case: the crucifixion of Jesus. It was predestined that Jesus die – he was the 'Lamb that was slain from the creation of the world' (Rev. 13:8). God also predestined the means that brought this to pass – 'with the help of wicked men' (Acts 2:23).

Satan prompted Judas Iscariot before his betrayal of Jesus (John 13:2). It fulfilled Old Testament prophecy (Matt. 26:15; Zech. 11:12), vindicated Jesus' own words long before the event of the betrayal (John 6:70–71) and was confirmed by Jesus' high priestly prayer when he said of the Twelve, 'None has been lost except the one doomed to destruction so that Scripture would be fulfilled' (John 17:12). Nothing takes God by surprise; the same God who predestined the end – the death of Jesus – predestined the means – those who conspired to kill him.

This was the faith of the earliest Church. When they were threatened further they prayed and reminded God of their persecution, noted what Herod and Pilate had done to conspire together, adding, 'They did what your power and will had *decided beforehand* should happen' (Acts 4:28). This is what kept them going – God is sovereign!

Have you thought about the way Jesus introduced his

parables? The way to understand the parables is to grasp the sovereignty of God. In introducing the parables he told why he spoke in parables:

> Though seeing, they do not see; though hearing, they do not hear or understand . . . Otherwise they might see with their ears, understand with their hearts and turn, and I would heal them. (Matt. 13:13–15)

The purpose of the parables, said Jesus, is to keep those who will not be saved from being saved – or healed. Parables were to keep those for whom they *are* intended to wait until the right time for them to have them unveiled. Parables were actually designed to keep certain people in the dark! This aspect of the teachings of Jesus has been largely neglected by the Church. We all know that Jesus spoke in parables but seem to sweep under the carpet his own rationale for using them. His reason for using them was his own belief in the sovereignty of God.

To be totally candid, I don't know how people cope with any other concept of God. Who would want to pray to a God who was not in total control? And yet some church leaders on both sides of the Atlantic have flirted with an idea which I can only call sub-Christian that maintains God does not know the future, that he waits for us to know what to do next and has no absolute assurance that he will win out. Indeed, one of the leading theologians from Canada who upholds this view of God was asked, 'How do you know for certain that Jesus Christ will win in the end? Does not your very theology leave open the possibility that God might not win in the end?' To give him full marks for being consistent, he agreed. And yet there were church leaders who applauded the notion.

The God of the Bible is sovereign, has a mind of his own, knows what is going to happen because he has declared the end from the beginning! Yes, said Isaiah, 'I make known the end from the beginning, from ancient times, what is still to come. I say: My purpose will stand, and I will do all that I please' (Isa. 46:10). This reminds me of a friend of mine whose six-year-old son knelt at his bedside and prayed, 'God bless Daddy and Mummy and me and, oh yes, please take care of yourself because if anything happens to you we are going to be in an awful mess.' If God is not sovereign, there is no hope that our Lord Jesus will triumph in the end as he did when God raised him from the dead.

I will now define what I mean by sovereignty of God: it is God's *authority* to do what he pleases with whomever he wills whenever he chooses. He does not need to explain himself, he is answerable to nobody. The key verse to me is Exodus 33:19, which came as God's response to Moses' request to see the glory of God: 'I will have mercy on whom I will have mercy, and I will have compassion on whom I will have compassion.' God blesses whom he chooses, withholding judgment (which is what mercy is) from those who deserve it and bestowing grace (undeserved favour) on those who don't deserve it.

Here are ten passages that have further and utterly convinced me of the sovereignty of God. I do not list these in the order in which they came to me in my theological development, neither are they listed with any priority of importance in mind. I begin with Matthew and work through the New Testament. To me they are all equal.

1 'No-one knows the Son except the Father, and no-one knows the Father except the Son and those to whom the Son chooses to reveal him' (Matt.11:27)

These words of Jesus are strong. If this were the only passage like this we have we would be tempted to say that 'the buck stops with him'; that is, Jesus. Jesus chooses who gets to know the Father. The first part of this extraordinary verse that says nobody knows the Son except the Father, and 'no-one knows the Father except the Son' indicates an exclusive relationship in the Godhead between the Father and the Son. Nobody gets in on it unless the Son – Jesus – selects someone who is privileged to know the Father. This verse simply means that knowing the Father and the Son is 'by invitation only' and the Son does the inviting. There is a similar passage in Luke 10:22.

2 'Yet to all who received him, to those who believed in his name, he gave the right to become children of God – children born not of natural descent, nor of human decision or a husband's will, but born of God' (John 1:12–13)

The one who gave the 'right' was the Lord Jesus, the Word made flesh. John then makes a theological comment on why these people were enabled to receive the Lord in the first place: they were born of God. God did it. It was not the result of having parents who were regenerate (as if to say being born in a Christian home doesn't make you a Christian), it is not an act of the will (as if to say becoming a Christian is not something you can do by yourself), or of a husband's will (your spouse can't make you a Christian). It is what God does – by being born of the Spirit. You did not do anything to cause your *natural* birth; you did not choose to be born. So also with your *spiritual* birth; being born of God is what God made happen.

3 'All that the Father gives me will come to me, and whoever comes to me I will never drive away' (John 6:37)

These are the words of Jesus. Whereas in Matthew 11:27 he takes the responsibility for who is privileged to know the Father, in this verse he says that the Father gives his Son a people. He does not say who they are or how many they are; only that, whoever they are, they will sooner or later come to Jesus. This line of thought is echoed in his prayer in John 17:6: 'I have revealed you to those whom *you* gave me out of the world . . . *you* gave them to me and they have obeyed your word'. In this case he must mean the Twelve (save for Judas – see John 17:12). But he goes on to say there will be more who will believe. All those who believe do so because they were given to the Son by the Father. As for those that come to him will never be driven away, this certainly means that those who come to Jesus will not be rejected; it may also mean that they will be kept because the words literally mean they won't be 'cast out'.

4 'No-one can come to me unless the Father who sent me draws him, and I will raise him up at the last day' (John 6:44)

These words of Jesus indicate that no person is able to come to the Father except 'by invitation only'. In fact they could not come unless the Holy Spirit drew them and in this instance the Father takes the responsibility for the work of the Spirit. It shows man's natural state of inability to give oneself life. One is born 'dead' according to Ephesians 2:1, 5, which means one has no natural ability to make a move unless one is given life first. This means that regeneration produces faith, not the other way around. Regeneration means that we have been quickened – given life. This is what enables a person to believe and why faith is God's own gift (Eph. 2:8–9). The bottom line: it is the Holy Spirit who gives life, which leads to faith and repentance. A person is unable to respond to the gospel unless the Holy Spirit is present to grant the hearer life.

5 'When the Gentiles heard this, they were glad and honoured the word of the Lord; and all who were appointed for eternal life believed' (Acts 13:48)

It is the last part that is quite remarkable: as many as were appointed ('ordained', AV) to eternal life believed. It would have been true had Luke said, 'All who believed were appointed to eternal life.' But Luke was now injecting his own theology into what had happened; you could say he was editorialising about the event of these Gentiles who were saved. Many sincere

Christians may understandably wish Luke had not said that or, at least, that he would have said, 'All who believed were ordained to eternal life' and yet that would have been a truism since it was well established that all who believe on Jesus are promised eternal life. But Luke has election and predestination in mind when he throws in this theological point of view. My Greek teacher at seminary admitted that the Greek is clear, he simply said to me, 'I disagree with Luke on this.' But he admitted that this was right there in the Bible. Agree or disagree, this is a strong affirmation of the sovereignty of God.

6 'Paul and his companions travelled throughout the region of Phrygia and Galatia, having been kept by the Holy Spirit from preaching the word in the province of Asia. When they came to the border of Mysia, they tried to enter Bithynia, but the Spirit of Jesus would not allow them to' (Acts 16:6–7)

These verses demonstrate the sovereignty of the Holy Spirit. Jesus spoke of the sovereignty of the Spirit when he said to Nicodemus, 'The wind blows wherever it pleases. You hear its sound, but you cannot tell where it comes from or where it is going. So is everyone born of the Spirit' (John 3:8). It is marvellous that Paul and his friends were governed by the Holy Spirit in all they did. There are two ways of looking at these verses; either Paul and his friends were consciously being governed by the Spirit and they felt definitely led to turn from Asia or move away from Bithynia, or Luke was editorialising again and attributing their being stopped as being a sovereign, providential overruling of the Spirit. In either case it shows God's prerogative to do what he pleases with whomever he pleases whenever he pleases.

7 'And those he predestined, he also called; those he called, he also justified; those he justified, he also glorified' (Rom. 8:30)

The Puritan William Perkins referred to this verse as the 'golden chain of redemption'. It is the theological biography of every believer – the stages one passes through from the time of conversion until one arrives in heaven. What makes the verse clearer is to ask: what must happen to a person before they can be glorified? Answer: that they were justified. What qualifies a person for being justified? Answer: that they were called. What must be true before a person can be called? Answer: that they were predestined. If one has been predestined, which means the person is called 'elect' or 'chosen', that person will eventually be glorified. All who are predestined will be called – which refers to the work of the Holy Spirit as in the case of John 6:44 above – sooner or later. And those who are called – theologians sometimes call this 'effectual calling' since there is always ultimate success in the Holy Spirit's efforts to produce saving faith with the predestined, or elect will come to faith and be justified. All those who are justified will be glorified – an implicit proof of the teaching 'once saved, always saved'. The bottom line: those predestined by God – what Luke refers to as being appointed to eternal life – will eventually be called, justified and glorified.

8 'Just as it is written: "Jacob I loved, but Esau I hated." What then shall we say? Is God unjust? Not at all! For he says to Moses, "I will have mercy on whom I will have mercy, and I will have compassion on whom I have compassion." It does not, therefore, depend on man's desire or effort, but on God's mercy' (Rom. 9:13–16)

These are probably the strongest words of all. I think it is fair to say that the word 'hate' may be understood as 'loved less'. But the fact remains that Paul wanted to establish that Jacob and Esau – 'before the twins were born or had done anything good or bad – in order that God's purpose in election might stand' (v. 11) – were set in God's purpose before they were born. It rules out the notion of foreseen faith, a teaching I will refer to in the next paragraph. Paul's main point, however, is this: being saved, justified, born again or converted – whatever term you wish to apply – does not depend on our desire or effort; being a Christian is an incalculable privilege and is granted to us entirely because of God's mercy. God gives this mercy to whom he gives this mercy – it is his sovereign right, his prerogative. Paul is not making a case that Esau is eternally lost in hell. Martin Luther (who believed in predestination) even said he expects to see Esau in heaven. Paul just wants to show that, if God can choose Jacob over Esau regarding the issue of inheritance even before either were born, he has the right to choose who receives mercy to this very day. Therefore nobody can take any credit for being a Christian; it is owing to the sheer goodness and mercy of God. Nothing more. For God is sovereign and has this right.

9 'Who has saved us and called us to a holy life – not because of anything we have done but because of his own purpose and grace. This grace was given us in Christ Jesus before the beginning of time' (2 Tim. 1:9)

This verse coheres with Ephesians 1:4–5,11 (please read) and further makes the point that God's choice of those who become Christians was not based upon good works – or foreseen faith. Some valiantly try to make the doctrine of predestination refer to what God knew in advance – that he knew who would believe and who wouldn't so he chose those he knew would believe. This is *nice* and softens the blow to a teaching that is difficult to understand. The problem is, Paul rules out this idea – both here and in Romans 9:11 (which we looked at above). Some picture God as being up high on a tall building and looking down on a parade and seeing the end of the parade – both the end and the beginning. It is reckoned that in this way God knew who would believe and chose them in advance of their being born. This teaching is known as Arminianism, named for Jacobus Arminius (1560–1609) who opposed Calvinism, named for John Calvin (1509–1564). Since the early seventeenth century, Protestantism has been generally divided between those who are Calvinists (e.g. George Whitefield, Jonathan Edwards, Charles H. Spurgeon) and Arminians (e.g. John Wesley, virtually all the early Methodists, Pentecostals and Charismatics). The bottom line: Paul says that God's choice of us was not based on anything we had done but by his grace alone – and that the choice was made before time began.

**10 'They stumble because they disobey the
message – which is also what they were destined
for. But you are a chosen people, a royal
priesthood, a holy nation . . . Once you were not
a people, but now you are the people of God;
once you had not received mercy, but now you
have received mercy' (1 Pet. 2:8–10)**

This is a very important passage, which shows the distinction
between those who are chosen and those who are not – the
latter are seen as disobedient. Whereas the elect are chosen
without any reference to worthiness, those not saved 'stumble
because they disobey the message'. It comes to this: if we are
saved it is because of the sheer grace and mercy of God; if we
are lost it is because we are disobedient to the message of the
gospel. If you ask: what about those who never hear the gospel?
my reply is that they will be judged by a different standard;
namely, the light of creation (Rom. 1) and conscience (Rom.
2). But there is no promise such people will be saved, only
judged by a different standard. But woe indeed to those who
have heard the gospel and rejected it. If, however, we are
justified by faith it is because we were chosen and called; if we
remain in our sins it is because we loved darkness rather than
light (John 3:19). Those who are lost will get what they deserve
– a just judgment; those who are saved receive what they don't
deserve – grace. Some get what they deserve. Yes, some get
what they don't deserve. That is why it is called 'grace'. 'For it
is by grace you have been saved, through faith – and this not
from yourselves, it is the gift of God – not by works, so that
no-one can boast' (Eph. 2:8–9).

I used to have friendly but none the less heated quarrels with my teachers and professors at seminary years ago. They were virtually all Arminians at that time. I was seen as the 'resident Calvinist' among the student body. I will never forget the answer given by the top Greek professor who did claim to follow the apostle Paul when I asked: 'If Paul believed what *I* think he truly believed how else *could* he have said it?' He replied, and I admired his candour, 'What he said is the only way he could have said it' had he believed what I was maintaining. So there were both professors at my old seminary who said they disagreed with what was written in the New Testament in the first place, and those who admitted that they did not want to believe what Paul said so they interpreted him according to their own bias.

What I have written in this chapter is not easy for some to accept. This is obviously because of the implication that not all are chosen. Why aren't all chosen? You tell me. I wish they were. I would have no objection if that were true; and I will be thrilled beyond words to find out one day that I have got it wrong. For if all were chosen, then all would be saved. This is known as 'universalism' – the belief of some that God is too kind to let anybody go to hell; therefore he will ensure that all will be saved in the end. I wish it were true – oh, how I wish this. But the God of the Bible does not reveal himself in such a manner that we can make a sound doctrine out of it. I wish he were that nice.

I have made a decision I am at ease with. To love and worship the God of the Bible and to defend him to the hilt. I love him. How could you? some ask. I answer: because I have had a glimpse of his glory and the little bit I have seen of him is so wonderful that I am prepared to say that what I don't understand about him will be even more glorious. If you opt for the Nice God you can be comfortable with, I would lovingly caution that you could be playing into Feurerbach's hands and projecting a God on the backdrop of the universe that coheres with your own idea about him but which is not the true God after all.

But maybe you don't want to accept the God of the Bible? That is a choice one must make. If Feuerbach's reasoning is valid, one reason I know that the God of the Bible is the true God is because Feuerbach never would have imagined that anyone would project the God I am describing in this book on the backdrop of the universe. Nobody would have come up with a God like this – he is too full of awe and, yes, terrible. 'For the LORD thy God is among you, a mighty God and terrible' (Deut. 7:21, AV; cf. Deut. 10:17; Neh. 1:5; 4:14; 9:32). The NIV never uses the word 'terrible' but rather 'awesome'. Yes, God is awesome. But whereas the word 'terrible' often means negative things we certainly would not want to say about God, the word 'awesome' has come to mean what is also very complimentary, thrilling and exciting. In a word: Feuerbach did not have a sovereign God in mind when he conceived of his rationale for being an atheist.

If the teaching in this chapter is new to you or difficult to accept you will probably want to know how the free offer of the gospel comes into play. For example, Jesus said that 'whoever believes in him shall not perish but have eternal life' (John 3:16). Paul said, 'Everyone who calls on the name of the Lord will be saved' (Rom. 10:13). Indeed, 'Whoever is thirsty, let him come; and whoever wishes, let him take the free gift of the water of life' (Rev. 22:17). The answer is: the offer is made to all in order that those whom God had chosen will respond. The task of the evangelist is not to figure out who has been chosen but to try to get everybody saved; the elect alone will hear the word so as to respond in saving faith. Those who are 'thirsty' and who 'call' on the name of the Lord show that God has called them or they would not come to Christ in faith.

If you ask, 'How do I know I have been chosen?', the answer is: 'Are you trusting Christ and not your good works to save you?' If the answer is 'Yes', be assured that you have been chosen, called and justified – and will be glorified. The great Charles Spurgeon used to say, 'Don't ask, "Am I elected?" Ask, "Do I believe?" '

Spurgeon fought those in his day who took an extreme view of the sovereignty of God and did little or nothing to preach the gospel to the lost. Some did not even believe in the free offer of the gospel. Some were more worried about false professions being made by people not really converted than they were the lost going to hell. Hence when a young preacher rushed up to Spurgeon after the latter was teaching these men to plead with sinners and do all you can to win the lost, he said, 'But Mr Spurgeon, what if we save one of the non-elect?' whereupon Spurgeon patted him on the shoulder and replied, 'Don't worry, my boy. God will forgive you for that.'

When we were out in the streets of Victoria in London giving out tracts and doing all we could to see the lost saved, I would say to our Pilot Lights, 'Speak to them as though their destiny were in your hands.' I would rather regret trying too hard than being passive in the matter of soul-winning. I used to hear a sweet old man pray week after week at our prayer meetings on Sunday evenings before the service, 'Lord, bring in thine elect tonight.' But Spurgeon, no slave to a rigid system and in no theological straitjacket, would pray, 'Lord, save all thine elect and then elect some more.'

The sovereignty of God, rightly understood and applied, does not militate against zealous evangelism; it is a corrective to those who go too far in trying to make the Holy Spirit do things – as we will see below.

This teaching, rightly understood and applied, then, as we shall see further in the following chapter, does not jeopardise evangelism, neither does it cut across one's need to know that they are eternally saved. Do not let those who have abused the teaching put you off from the solid, clear, biblical teaching we are attempting to uphold in this book.

Nobody is rejected who trusts the blood of Jesus. For that blood was shed for all (2 Cor. 5:15; Heb. 2:9). Do not worry whether you are chosen, only worry whether your trust is in the blood shed on the cross. If your reliance and only hope is in Christ's blood, you are as saved and secure as the apostle Paul himself. Nobody – nobody – is turned down who puts their trust in what Jesus did for them on the cross. And yet those who do so show that God has chosen them.

5

Why Believe in the Sovereignty of God?

'When the pure gospel is preached to people as they are it will save some and condemn others, but it will accomplish God's purpose'

Henry Mahan

Why is this chapter important? Why should you and I believe in the sovereignty of God as I have briefly outlined so far? The main reason, apart from the obvious reason – to be in line with God's own Word – is that this teaching is a needed corrective to so many abuses that are rampant in the Church today, speaking generally. I will give the following examples.

1 Manipulative evangelism

This has been done both in public appeals – high-pressured altar calls – and in personal evangelism when a person is button-holed and coerced to make a profession of faith without any persuasion in the heart. 'A man convinced against his will is of the same opinion still', someone said. How true. Some seem to think that any profession of faith, or even baptism, proves that the person has been converted.

I happen to believe in personal evangelism. Our Pilot Light ministry at Westminster Chapel was entirely that, talking to people – total strangers – in the streets between Victoria Station and Buckingham Palace about Jesus. Moreover, we did all we could to lead them to Christ once the gospel was presented to them. We have given away tens of thousands of pamphlets in nearly 30 languages. No doubt many who made professions of faith were not converted. But some of them were. One of them went into the Anglican ministry.

We will not know until we get to heaven how many people were led to a saving knowledge of Christ through our Pilot Light ministry. But it is personal evangelism. I did my best to be governed by the sovereignty of God in our evangelism and cautioned our Pilot Lights not to say, 'Five people were saved today' but rather to say, 'Five people prayed to receive the Lord Jesus today.' Only God knows who is saved. We made sure that no Pilot Light (that we knew of) pressured people to make a decision. I taught a ten-week course on street witnessing – several of the weeks dealt with theology – and emphasised the absolute necessity of the work of the Holy Spirit in evangelism.

Evangelistic preaching that is followed by public appeals has sometimes done a lot of harm. The reason 'altar calls' were not given at Westminster Chapel before I came was based on a sincere concern not to usurp the Spirit's work in persuading a person to become a Christian. When I started giving appeals at the Chapel in June 1982 I made sure there was no pressure, such as singing twenty verses of 'Just as I am' or 'Almost persuaded'. I even wrote a book called *Stand Up and Be Counted*, which makes a case for giving appeals within the context of the sovereign work of the Holy Spirit.

I have watched how evangelists, even pastors, play into the emotions of people to get them to 'walk the aisle' and make a public decision for Christ. The most reprehensible thing of all is to give the impression that these people who walk the aisle, join a church, sign a card or get baptised are actually converted. This would make God nice indeed. Nice God would not require people to be convicted of their sins by the Holy Spirit and make their calling and election sure by holy living (2 Pet. 1:10).

Only the Holy Spirit can convert a man or woman; getting people to make a public decision without the inward persuasion of the Spirit is manipulation and abuse. It is nice preachers making God look nice by promising them a home in heaven – whether their hearts have been changed or not. 'Just come forward, let us baptise you', so your name can be added to the list of our many church members and can make statistics look good. This abuse of God's holy Name grieves the Spirit. The Dove flutters away and nobody feels a thing. God is too nice to upset the vast programme of the Church.

On the other hand, it seems to me that it is quite right to encourage people to respond to what they have heard – to allow them to do what they *want* to do, not what they don't want to do. Peter did this after his sermon on the day of Pentecost when Luke says, 'With many other words he warned them; and he pleaded with them, "Save yourselves from this corrupt generation" ' (Acts 2:40).

In J.I. Packer's classic book *Evangelism and the Sovereignty of God* the author employs the word 'antinomy' – parallel principles that seem irreconcilable but are both true. The Bible is full of them – Jesus is God and man, the Christian is simultaneous saint and sinner, God is merciful and just. Our call in evangelism is to reach all we can as long as we can but to remember this unwavering principle: only God saves. It is an antinomy.

When we are governed by the sovereignty of God we will find it makes all the difference in what we try to get people to do. You cannot save the non-elect and you will not dislodge God's chosen. The preaching of the gospel will save some and condemn others, but it will accomplish God's purpose. New Testament evangelism stands in stark contrast to the Nice God who would not offend anyone.

2 The promise of prosperity

One of the strongest movements in some parts of the Church at the present time is largely associated with an emphasis on what is often called the 'prosperity gospel'. This view suggests that it is the will of God for every Christian to be prosperous. Not just spiritually prosperous but financially blessed as well.

This message has great appeal, especially to poor people. One can appreciate how struggling families welcome a way out of their financial difficulties. When a preacher comes along and preaches prosperity to them – telling them it is God's will – such people will naturally say, 'Yes, I want this.' Such people are usually told that they must show faith in God if they want this prosperity to come to them, and the way to demonstrate that faith is to send money to the very preacher who presents them with the good news of prosperity. They almost never say, 'Give your money to someone else, not me', but always to their very ministry.

One can appreciate why people send in their money; they want to show God they really believe in him. Often the preachers who appeal for people's money in this fashion are themselves very prosperous indeed – it is shown by the clothes they wear, the gold jewellery on them and the cars they drive, not to mention their luxurious homes. Instead of putting people off it often has the opposite effect; desperate people think, 'This must be right because this preacher seems so successful' – and they give sacrificially.

What worries me most is that such preaching plays into people's greed. Greed is something you get naturally, not by taking a course in university on how to be greedy. It is a part of the sinful flesh we inherited from our first parents after their original sin in the Garden of Eden. The apostle Paul put greed alongside sexual immorality (Eph. 5:3). When we watch television entertainers play into our sexual appetites we are not surprised; we take that for granted. But for Christian leaders to play into our greed in order to persuade us to part with our money is, in my opinion, wicked.

But is not the teaching of prosperity in the Bible? Yes, it is. It was a part of the Mosaic Law. The blessings for obedience are quite wonderful. (Read Deut. 28:1–14.) But the promise of blessing was not based on sacrificial giving to a ministry but to adherence to the whole Law of God. Prosperity, then, was promised to the godly – for obedience to the Law.

The blessing that is promised on the basis of financial giving was on tithing – which was to be given to the 'storehouse' (Mal. 3:8–10). I have written a book called *Tithing* – reissued as *The Gift of Giving* – making the case that the New Testament equivalent to the 'storehouse' is the local church. In a word: the tithe, one tenth of your income, should be given to your own church. I go further and make the case that you cannot outgive the Lord and should give to Christian charities beyond your tithe apart from your church if you like – so long as the initial tithe was given to your church. (Some missionary organisations weren't very happy with this as they wanted church members to give tithes directly to them.) Malachi 3:10 made a bold promise:

'Bring the whole tithe into the storehouse, that there may be food in my house. Test me in this,' says the LORD Almighty, 'and see if I will not throw open the floodgates of heaven and pour out so much blessing that you will not have room enough for it.'

But note: it was to be given to the storehouse.

It would appear that the overwhelming thrust of prosperity gospel teaching is from church leaders who want people to give to the ministries of those church leaders. If they are wanting their hearers to enjoy prosperity because this is God's will, why don't they exhort their hearers to give to their own church? Were they to do this, one would see that it is the glory of God and the building up of the saints that such people were interested in. But that does not seem to be the case.

But the main point I want to make is this. There is no categorical promise in the New Testament that God wants you to prosper and that not to prosper is due to your own lack of faith. I do believe that in the long run we cannot outgive the Lord (see 2 Cor. 9:6–9). But to say that 'God wants you to be well off financially or to prosper materially on the condition you will send us your money' is to cross over a line that shows contempt for the sovereignty of God. The most one should promise is that God may prosper you. But God is sovereign. He cannot be controlled. To use his Name to get people to give to one's ministry with the promise 'You will be prosperous' is to manipulate people and offer them hope that is beyond what God's Word guarantees.

Paul said,

> I know what it is to be in need, and I know what it is to have plenty. I have learned the secret of being content in any and every situation, whether well fed or hungry, whether living in plenty or in want. (Phil. 4:11–12)

Preaching that godliness with contentment is great gain (1 Tim. 6:6) honours God and enables people to build up a reward in heaven. He promises prosperity in this life . . . to some – those who can be trusted with great riches. But not all. The promise is, 'I will have mercy on whom I will have mercy.' Let the prosperity gospel ministers be gripped by God's sovereignty, and see what their preaching would be like after that.

3 Healing

The prosperity gospel is often associated with the ministry of healing. Perhaps unfairly many refer to the 'health and wealth' gospel. The premiss is something like this: God wants you to be healthy and wealthy; he wants you to be rich and he wants you to be healed if you are unwell.

I doubt Paul would have gone into Corinth with fear and trembling as he did had he authority to promise that all sick people will be healed and nobody need be in financial difficulty if they will accept Jesus. No need to fear with a message like that! People would flock to receive such a Jesus. No stigma, no offence. They would queue up to get their healing and assurance of prosperity.

But knowing the offence of the cross as he did, Paul none the less determined 'to know nothing while I was with you except Jesus Christ and him crucified' (1 Cor. 2:2). By this Paul meant that faith in Jesus meant that wisdom, righteousness, holiness and redemption was put to our credit (1 Cor. 1:30). We were declared righteous before God and saved from the wrath to come. That was Paul's gospel. Not a word about healing. To find a people that would be interested in such a gospel required the anointing of the Spirit on his preaching. That anointing came but Paul underneath was aware of his own frailties.

Paul believed in healing. He was an instrument of the Holy Spirit in seeing people healed many times. But he did not claim that the blood shed on the cross *guaranteed* that those who trust Jesus would not only be saved but also healed.

But God has become very nice in recent times, according to

some. Nice indeed. We are now told by some – often the same preachers who promise prosperity – that when Jesus died on the cross it was for our being healed of all diseases. That if we are not healed it is because of our lack of faith.

I long to hear one of these preachers uphold the real reason Jesus died: to save us from our sins, to ensure that we will get to heaven, not hell, when we die; to clothe us with the righteousness of Jesus, to free us from the demands of the Mosaic Law, to bring us into intimacy with God the Father and to enable us to have communion with the Holy Spirit. This is Paul's gospel.

But it is hard to get people motivated to send in their money for this. It is far more interesting to learn that 'God wants you healed' than it is 'God wants to save you from your sins'. So Paul went into Corinth with fear and trembling because he knew this was not what people were interested in hearing. But he stuck to his guns, stayed with the preaching of the cross – 'foolishness to those who are perishing, but to us who are being saved it is the power of God' (1 Cor. 1:18).

I watch some of these preachers who offer health and prosperity over television. They quote verses in the Bible, yes. But they often astonishingly miss the main point of the gospel – and never, ever, seem to get around to preaching the real reason Jesus died on the cross. You get the impression that the reason he died was for what we can enjoy here on this planet in the here and now. Existentialist teaching – what's in it for me – has found its way into the Church, largely through television, and the gospel itself has passed behind a cloud. Whatever happened to the gospel?

When Isaiah prophesied that the death of Messiah would

mean we would be healed by his wounds (Isa. 53:5), he promised that the Son of God would heal people. And he did. Yes, Jesus of Nazareth did just that. The miracles were so vast that 'even the whole world would not have room for the books that would be written' (John 21:25). Not only that; we have the promise of Isaiah that foretold this. For when demon-possessed or the physically ill were brought to Jesus, and they were delivered and healed, Matthew quotes Isaiah: 'He took up our infirmities and carried our diseases' (Matt. 8:17; Isa. 53:4).

But this aspect of Jesus' ministry is almost the only thing some church leaders wish to focus on. They choose the part of Jesus' life and teachings that appeals to a generation that is interested in comfort in the here and now. It is a nice God who gives people – who otherwise have little time for the true gospel – what plays into their comfort zones.

J.I. Packer has referred to the Bible belt in America as being a thousand miles wide and one inch thick. That Bible belt would not be there at all had there not been at least two Great Awakenings – in New England in the eighteenth century and in the South in the early nineteenth century. Those revivals, which led to countless others all over the United States, were characterised by the preaching of the cross, the need to be ready to meet God because there is a heaven and a hell, and the changing of people's lives from promiscuous to being godly. The Bible belt today may be a shadow of what it once was but that is partly because the preaching of today is almost a different gospel – or, at least, a lop-sided interest in the things of God for the wrong reasons.

Never forget that the apostle Paul had a 'thorn in the flesh'. We do not know what it was – whether it was physical or had to do with illness at all. But the fact remains that even he – God's sovereign and highly esteemed vessel – prayed three times (2 Cor. 12:8) for it to be removed! God merely replied, 'My grace is sufficient for you' (2 Cor. 12:9). Paul knew that God was sovereign and could give or withhold mercy and would be just in acting either way. And yet one prominent 'health and wealth' television preacher actually said, believe it or not, 'If the apostle Paul had had my faith he wouldn't have had his thorn in the flesh.' Think about that.

I believe in healing. I believe God heals today. In this book I tell the story of my wife's own miraculous healing. For I do not believe that the miraculous ended after the early Church gave us the Bible. 'Jesus Christ is the same yesterday, today and for ever' (Heb. 13:8). In Westminster Chapel we had regular healing services and saw genuine healings from time to time.

But God is sovereign in healing as he is in salvation. It is not right to put sick people under a cloud of guilt because they have not been healed. That is what so many faith healers do today. I love what Randy Clark said; namely, that in the New Testament the people who were healed were not the ones required to have sufficient faith, it was the ones who did the praying. But this is not the emphasis with most healing ministries today, I am sorry to say. They put sick people under pressure to have more faith, and such weak people blame themselves for their sickness. This is so unfair and wrong.

The main reason Jesus died on the cross was to prepare us for heaven. All who trust his blood for salvation will be saved and guaranteed a home in heaven, but not all who trust Christ's blood are healed. Salvation was the primary purpose of Jesus' death, healing was subsidiary. But the kind of preachers I am describing in this chapter make the secondary reason for the cross the main reason. Why? You tell me. It is not the real gospel, it is counterfeit. A nice God watches all this happen and such preachers never seem to feel a thing. No sense of shame. No apologies for making innocent, ill people feel guilty. I knew a godly, sincere man (I was his pastor) who depleted his life savings by sending all he had to a ministry that promised that it was the best way to be sure he would be healed. He sadly never was healed and soon died with nothing and left his widow virtually penniless.

Where is the preaching of the sovereignty of God among church leaders like this? I fear that it does not exist at all. Some would not believe it, for doing so would cause their ministries to disintegrate and come to shreds. For most of it is built on the premiss that you must show that you have faith by sowing seed for the harvest of healing. So people send in their money. And a nice God looks down from heaven, aching in his heart, but says nothing. For now.

I think a lot about the rise of faith healers that came when there really was a powerful anointing of healing abroad. Paul Cain told me that between 1949 and 1951 virtually everybody he prayed for was healed. Wheelchairs were stacked to the ceilings of auditoriums and tents in which he ministered. But that anointing, for some reason, lifted. Paul Cain himself became a recluse and decided to wait for the day that, just maybe, God would do it again. But others in such a ministry kept it up and would not concede that his powerful anointing wasn't around as it was. They then started blaming the sick people for their lack of faith if they weren't healed, and threw in the prophecy of Isaiah 53 to prove that healing was as inherent in the atonement as the promise of salvation. So sad. So wrong. People wanted a nice God who never says 'No' and who does not have a sovereign will.

We need a restoration of the sovereignty of God in the Church today. Let God be God. He is able to heal, but he may not choose to heal. He is sovereign. Even Jesus himself walked right past the lame man at the temple gate called Beautiful many times over the years and did not heal this man. It would seem Jesus saved him for Peter and John who came along later and saw this man gloriously healed (Acts 3). The point is, Jesus himself – who had all authority and power – walked past the man and left him unhealed. He mirrored the sovereignty of God in his ministry as does the Holy Spirit to this day.

The preaching and teaching of the sovereignty of God, were they to emerge all over the Church, would encourage us to believe that:

1 God is alive and real;
2 he has a will of his own which is to be respected; and
3 we do not need to feel guilty when things don't happen as we would wish.

The discovery of the sovereignty of God is a wonderful recipe for overcoming guilt.

Perhaps God will revive the anointing of healing in great power once again. If he does, let us never forget that he who gives can also take away – and be perfectly just either way.

4 Spiritual warfare

In recent years there has been a considerable interest in the subject of spiritual warfare, the demonic and deliverance. I know some people who have devoted the whole of their ministries to this. I ran into a casual acquaintance a few years ago and asked him what he is doing these days and he replied, 'I am into spiritual warfare. I'm doing spiritual warfare these days.' I wasn't sure what to say. I know what I thought: this man is playing with electricity with wet fingers and had better be very, very careful. I did not know him well enough to share my thoughts. I gather he gave it up later on.

A very high-profile preacher decided he would go into a famous city in California and attack the devil. He should have known he was out of his depth. Sadly he was not surrounded with prudent people to whom he was accountable. He marched into this city and started attacking powers and authorities, believing (I assume) he could make a difference and turn that city around. Instead he was completely defeated, overcome by the enemies he proposed to attack, humiliated and was out of the ministry weeks later.

Spiritual warfare is serious, serious business. God never promotes us to the level of our incompetence. The chapter on accepting the limits of our anointing in my book *The Anointing* is relevant here. Accepting our limits is humbling but always crucial and yet perhaps never so important as in the area of the demonic.

The devil is real, the demonic is real, demon possession is real and the attack of evil forces is ever present. Said Peter, 'Be self-controlled and alert. Your enemy the devil prowls around like a roaring lion looking for someone to devour' (1 Pet. 5:8). He is always prowling around waiting for an entry point in our lives by which he can turn things upside down, bring us to despair and make us think there is no way out.

The devil will be most happy for you to take either of these two options: first, do not believe in him at all – deny his existence entirely (he would love that); or second, become preoccupied with the demonic, the occult and go to extremes on spiritual warfare – taking the devil on, so to speak. He loves that too.

You are no match for the devil. By yourself. Don't ever take him on, don't ever pick a fight with him and don't ever imagine yourself so strong that you can punch him in the nose and make him leave you alone. He will not only love it, he will divert you from the things that ought to preoccupy you and you will become virtually useless in the kingdom of God. I am sorry, but that is the way it is.

What worries me most about certain people that I myself have come into contact with is this. They have a low view of the sovereignty of God and a high view of their knowledge of the devil. Some of them seem to concentrate on the devil more than they believe in the pre-eminent power of God, and sadly some don't seem to have much responsible fear of the devil whatever. They deal with him as if he were a toy to play with.

There are a number of Scriptures that have governed me in this area. I pray the Holy Spirit will apply these to your life and ministry.

Finally, be strong in the Lord and in his mighty power . . . For our struggle is not against flesh and blood, but against the rulers, against the authorities, against the powers of this dark world and against the spiritual forces of evil in the heavenly realms. (Eph. 6:10,12–13)

What is often forgotten about the verses that follow is the word 'stand'. Four times in Ephesians 6:11–14 comes this word 'stand'. Why? This leads me to the first principle of spiritual warfare I put to you:

1 Spiritual warfare is defensive

You stand. You don't jump. You don't run. You don't even walk. You certainly don't want to slip and fall. And you don't want to go backwards. 'After you have done everything, to stand.' Don't try to make progress. Just stand. Because when the 'day of evil' comes – and it will surely come – you make progress when you simply stand. Standing is progress when you are resisting the devil. Having told us that the devil is like a roaring lion, Peter said, 'Resist him' (1 Pet. 5:9). James also said it, 'Resist the devil, and he will flee from you' (Jas. 4:7). You can resist him only when he attacks. Resisting someone means that they have attacked you. You don't run around resisting what isn't already attacking you. The very point of resistance is that it is defensive. That means being defensive as opposed to going on the offence.

2 Don't ever attack the devil

You wait for him to attack. If he never attacks, wonderful! Be glad. Don't lament. Consider that God is answering your prayer (if you pray it as you should), 'Lead us not into temptation, but deliver us from the evil one' (Matt. 6:13). The reason spiritual warfare is defensive is because you are not promised grace if you are on the attack but only if you follow the Word of God – and resist the devil when he does attack. If you do the attacking, believe me, you will have a fight on your hands too big for you. You are no match for the devil. But you will quote Jesus' words, 'When someone stronger [than the devil] attacks and overpowers him, he [Jesus] takes away the armour in which the man trusted and divides up the spoils' (Luke 11:22). But this assumes you have been attacked first; then you have the promise of God's presence and protection.

In a word: wait for the devil to attack before you attack. Some people are clever but not wise. Paul showed wisdom when he did not immediately turn to the slave girl who was tantalising the disciples. She kept saying, 'These men are servants of the Most High God, who are telling you the way to be saved.' This sounds good, doesn't it? The Puritan William Perkins used to say, 'Don't believe the devil even when he tells the truth.'

> [This girl] kept this up for many days. Finally Paul became so troubled that he turned around and said to the spirit, 'In the name of Jesus Christ I command you to come out of her!' At that moment the spirit left her. (Acts 16:18)

He waited many days. Too many don't wait; they go on the attack at once and get in over their depth.

3 Be sure you know the Lord Jesus

As we saw in the Introduction, some Jews who went around driving out evil spirits tried to invoke the name of the Lord Jesus over those who were demon-possessed and would say, 'In the name of Jesus whom Paul preaches, I command you to come out.' On one occasion,

> the evil spirit answered them, 'Jesus I know, and I know about Paul, but who are you?' Then the man who had the evil spirit jumped on them and overpowered them all. He gave them such a beating that they ran out of the house naked and bleeding. (Acts 19:15–16)

This is what I mean by promoting yourself to the level of your incompetence. 'As thy days, so shall thy strength be' (Deut. 33:25, AV). Be sure you are called by the Spirit to get involved in this kind of ministry.

4 Don't rebuke the devil directly

You may say, 'But Jesus did.' I say: you aren't Jesus. I have watched sincere, good and well-meaning people say to the devil, 'I rebuke you' and keep on saying it. I don't think the devil is too threatened by your word. And if you aren't careful he will suddenly overwhelm you and leave you in shreds before you know what has happened. The most overlooked and neglected verse in the New Testament when it comes to spiritual warfare is in Jude 9: 'Even the archangel Michael, when he was disputing with the devil about the body of Moses, *did not dare to bring a slanderous accusation* against him, but said, "The Lord rebuke you!" ' Think about that verse. Michael was presumably the highest ranking and most qualified angel in the heavenly realms to take on the devil and rebuke him and give him a piece of his mind. But no. He calmly said, 'The Lord rebuke you.' I would plead for those involved in spiritual warfare to ponder this verse.

God is bigger than the devil. This ought to go without saying, but I would encourage all who read these lines to know that God is superior to the devil; he is sovereign and can with a little finger wipe him out before you can count to ten. And will do so one day. In the meantime remember that the devil goes only where God gives him permission. We learn this from Job. God took the initiative and let the devil have a go at Job but only let him go so far (Job 1:6–12). Whenever there is a presence of evil, whether it be an attack on you or your being near a demon-possessed person, do not panic. God let it happen. He did. The devil doesn't make a move without our Heavenly Father's permission. This is perhaps the main reason the teaching of the sovereignty of God is essential to balanced and effective spiritual warfare. Don't panic when you see evil. Lean on a sovereign God who can give you victory in an instant – if you follow the rules.

The teaching of the sovereignty of God is to me most edifying and comforting. If harm has come from the abuse of this teaching, so too has harm come from incompetent people who take on more than they should when it comes to spiritual warfare. This part of the book could save some people a lot of heartache.

5 Personal success

I need this part of the present section more than anybody I know. I will come clean with you. Though I believe to my fingertips every word I have typed above, I fail again and again in putting many of these principles into practice. I am too often the world's worst in applying so many of these principles.

Here is the verse that must grip you and me: 'No-one from the east or the west or from the desert can exalt a man. But it is God who judges: He brings one down, he exalts another' (Ps. 75:6–7). Of course it is true that people can come from the east and the west and exalt you or me. But not under the anointing of the ungrieved Spirit of God. Our problem is, we run ahead of God, think he is right there with us and approving all we say and do, only to discover later (sometimes years later) that what we did was in our strength and not God's. Which is why we got into difficulty.

If you read *In Pursuit of His Glory* you will know I used to be a door-to-door vacuum cleaner salesman. Only yesterday Louise and I drove up to South Miami and Coral Gables and I showed her the area where I used to knock on doors and sell to the rich and the super rich. I was a pretty good salesman. I could sometimes talk a person into trading in the vacuum cleaner they bought the week before on my new one – and buy a second one for their upstairs! It was the way my dad brought me up. I started selling *Grit*, the weekly newspaper, from house to house in Ashland, Kentucky, and came to be at home in knocking on strangers' doors. I have consequently been a highly driven man. Many of the marital problems Louise and I have had over the years is due to my drivenness. I was driven to prepare four sermons a week for twenty-five years in London; now I am driven to finish writing this book and am supposed to be living in retirement. It drives Louise almost mad.

For those who are driven (whatever the cause) or have a double dose of ambition, we can be believers in the sovereignty of God in our heads but deny these very principles in our hearts. I tried so hard to bring revival to Westminster Chapel. I tried too hard. Only God can bring revival; in the same way that only God can save and convert people by the Holy Spirit.

Whereas I never raised a finger to make things happen in order to become the pastor of a church (from my church in Palmer, Tennessee to Westminster Chapel), I tried too hard to make things happen once I became the minister.

You may be a businessperson, a physician, a secretary, a lorry driver, a computer whiz, a carpenter, a teacher or an architect. God has given you an anointing to get things done at the level of your natural competence without stress. Perhaps you are looking to make more money, to get the more prestigious position or possibly to change careers altogether. Remember these words: 'Unless the LORD builds the house, its builders labour in vain' (Ps. 127:1). Unless God is behind your goals, you will not succeed.

God was angry with ancient Israel for pursuing unjust goals. 'I was enraged by his sinful greed; I punished him, and hid my face in anger, yet he kept on in his wilful ways' (Isa. 57:17). 'Sinful greed' may be translated 'unjust goals'. Unjust goals are aspirations, aims or targets we have set for ourselves but which God did not set. When we envisage a target or goal that God did not put into our hearts, we may succeed, yes, but the fall-out isn't worth it. Broken health. Marriage break-up. Cold hearts. Failure as a parent. It is called 'winning the battle but losing the war'.

Here are principles I put to you as we bring this section of the book on the sovereignty of God to a close:

1 When it comes to the place of honour, take the lowest place

One of my favourite parables of Jesus is when he cautioned us not to go to the top table when invited to a banquet. This is because the host might have to say to you, 'Take a lower place' because someone more distinguished than you may have been invited and you will be humiliated! In order to save face, then, take the least prominent seat in the room and then, just maybe, you will be invited to move to a better place and be honoured in the presence of all your fellow guests. 'For everyone who exalts himself will be humbled, and he who humbles himself will be exalted' (Luke 14:11). I have had to ask myself many times, do I want to be exalted if it is not God's time – or do I want to be exalted if he does not want me to be exalted at all? My answer is 'No'. What use is it to be exalted before people and have everybody notice when I know in my heart that God the Father is not behind this and is not pleased? It is only a matter of time and the truth will be out! The humiliation later won't be worth it. God wants only what is best for us and our trying to make things happen to make ourselves look good will backfire on us if we do not let him do the exalting.

2 Avoid the love of money

It is called a 'root of all kinds of evil' and, indeed, some people, 'eager for money, have wandered from the faith and pierced themselves with many griefs' (1 Tim. 6:10). Some people can be trusted with a lot of money. I have always assumed I am not one of those people. I know that a long time ago – over forty years ago in fact – God dealt with me firmly that I was not to make a lot of money but that he would take care of me. That is the way it has been across the years. We have come to retirement after living carefully and without a lot of money over the years, and God has blessed us to exceed all expectations.

But there are those who are called to make money. Chances are, certainly if you are a Christian and walking in the Spirit, if you are called to make a lot of money it will be not because of a love for money you have but because you are motivated to accomplish extraordinary things. I have watched Christian businessmen who did have a love of money and watched them crash! Those the Lord loves he disciplines (Heb. 12:6). If you are governed by the love of money, you will pay dearly for it down the road. 'Godliness with contentment is great gain' (1 Tim. 6:6). If God blesses you financially, fall on your face and thank him and become a great giver to the Lord's work.

3 Don't defend yourself when you are criticised

Don't rob God of what he does 'best': the enterprise of vindicating those who are wronged. Everything God does is extremely good; you could say there is nothing he does best because nothing he does can be improved upon. But if I may be forgiven for putting it this way, what he does so brilliantly – the ways he does it boggle the mind – is to clear a person's name who has been falsely accused, lied about or hurt in any way. God is for the underdog and if you have been hurt, lied about, put down or mistreated, you got God's attention – then and there. The problem is, we tend to want to 'help him out'. Big mistake. He gets off our case before you can bat an eyelash. But when we will do nothing (yes, you read it correctly) but let him work on our behalf, we will be so glad we did. Don't necessarily expect vindication to come today or tomorrow but, if you have been the object of injustice, he took notice. Remember that the example of not giving up in praying was a widow who kept asking for justice (Luke 18:1–8). Bottom line: don't ever – ever – try to clear your own name. That's God's job.

4 Don't be overly concerned to explain yourself all the time

My friend Pete Cantrell always says, 'The greatest freedom is having nothing to prove.' I think too of Shakespeare's famous words, 'Methinks the lady doth protest too much.' This principle borders on the one above obviously, but is not always the same thing. Sometimes there is a case of making yourself clearer if you have been unclear or misunderstood. Sometimes I don't say things as clearly as I should, even when I write. I must not be defensive but take the criticism on board and set the person free who needs to know what I meant. On the other hand, we can be too occupied with what people think and lose all sense of liberty. 'Where the Spirit of the Lord is, there is freedom' (2 Cor. 3:17). When we have his smile and approval we must not trade them in for the approval of people. If it will set the other person free, explain yourself; but if it is only to make yourself look good, opt for the liberty of the Spirit instead.

5 Accept criticism without being defensive

'Blessed are the meek' (Matt. 5:5). Meekness is taking criticism without being angry, retorting or even covering up for yourself. Meekness is agreeing with the person's right to say what they say, understanding why they say it and even turning the other cheek (Matt. 5:39). After all, they may be right! There is usually a grain of truth to all criticism we receive, even when it is unfair. The least we can do is say, 'I see what you mean' and maybe it is time to say, 'You are right.' But never should we make the person feel bad for saying what they do. Being defensive in such a case is a dead giveaway that we are very insecure, so why give them that! Somerset Maugham said that when people ask for criticism, they really want praise. So true. When you accept criticism and compliments in much the same way, you are beginning to get free.

6 Earnestly seek the honour that comes from God alone

There are two verses that I have sought to be governed by in this connection; the first I have already mentioned in Chapter 3 – John 5:44: 'How can you believe if you accept praise from one another, yet make no effort to obtain the praise that comes from the only God?' In this significant verse Jesus reveals the real reason the Jews missed their Messiah – they were too enamoured with the praise of people. Note that Jesus said that they make no *effort* to obtain the praise (Greek, *doxa* – honour, glory, praise) that comes from God alone. We may not master the matter of not being concerned with the praise of people but we can certainly make an attempt! The second verse is Ecclesiastes 4:4: 'And I saw that all labour and all achievement spring from man's envy of his neighbour.' This verse shook me rigid one evening when I saw it clearly for the first time. It shows that what has been accomplished on our planet throughout the centuries and to the present time has been motivated by people wanting to make people jealous; therefore they get things done to get their admiration and their sense of envy. Surely we should strive to rise above that! Do you?

If this chapter grips you, it can be only the result of the power of the Spirit at work. You must know that the majority of people hate the truths of God's sovereignty. The things contained in this chapter could not possibly mean much to someone who is hostile to the principles of God's own personal glory but are enthralled instead with the glory of man, 'What's in it for me?' and an immediate reward. Therefore if you feel the Lord tapping you on the shoulder in these lines, I can assure you it is because he is communicating with you, trying to get your attention and wanting intimacy with you – as opposed to not telling the world that he is hungry (Ps. 50:12).

Let God be 'nice' to the world by not bothering to judge, to upset people, move them out of their comfort zones or stir them up for their lack of spiritual appetite or love for his interests.

But I don't want him to be nice to me. I would prefer, if necessary, for him to chasten or discipline me. I want to know what is on his heart, what moves him, what honours him and what gives him pleasure.

He owes you and me nothing. He gives mercy to whom he will. If he shows mercy to me by letting me know he is hungry, I will in gratitude fall at his feet. I repeat: if the Lord is putting a burning in your heart, don't let him move on as if he is finished with you; beg him to come and stay. You will never be sorry.

6

The 'Yuk' Factor

'But God chose the foolish things of the world to shame the
wise; God chose the weak things of the world to shame the
strong. He chose the lowly things of this world and the despised
things'

1 Cor. 1:27–28

I came to a conclusion years ago that God is on the lookout
for what will make sophisticated people say 'Yuk' when he is
ready to show his glory again on the earth. Why? Paul tells us.
God's glory is always related to nullifying our fleshly wisdom
in order to make room for what God calls wisdom – his glory.
Indeed, Paul said that he chose the lowly and despised things
in order that no one may boast – glory – before the Lord (1
Cor. 1:29). All I know is, nearly every time God does something
unusual it not only takes most people by surprise – whether it
be the person he chooses or the manner in which he chooses

145

to show up – but also makes the educated, cultured and high-powered of this world say, simply, 'Yuk' – an unsophisticated way of saying 'Surely not'. It is still what we often say or think when we have a feeling of disgust, revulsion or what is distasteful. Here is a passage that lies behind all that is to be said in this chapter:

'For my thoughts are not your thoughts, neither are your ways my ways,' declares the LORD. 'As the heavens are higher than the earth, so are my ways higher than your ways and my thoughts than your thoughts.' (Isa. 55:8–9)

The issue in this chapter is partly to answer those who say, 'That can't be God', when they come across an unusual or unprecedented manifestation that purports to be of divine origin or when a teaching springs forth that cuts across the way they had chosen to believe. Often our minds are made up and we don't want to be confused by any interpretation that threatens our comfort zone.

The thesis of this chapter is that God uses 'yuk factors' to promote his glory. If something can make you say 'Yuk', or 'Surely not', be careful because God in heaven may just look down and say, 'Good. This will work.' Perhaps it emerges something like this: behind the scenes there is a Trinitarian conference in the heavenlies where it is determined what is the next thing that will cause smug people to say 'Yuk'. As Paul Cain used to put it, 'God offends the mind to reveal the heart.'

Why is this chapter important? First, God is a God of glory and will not cater to our sophistication. That which is highly esteemed, or highly valued, among men and women is an abomination in the sight of God (Luke 16:15). In other words, if religious people generally think something is worthy of being regarded as meriting the term 'excellence', chances are that it makes God sick. He finds it detestable. Second, it is often the case that what religious people criticise most is the very thing God is in and the very thing of which he was the architect. Keep your ear to the ground and take note of the things which religious people find fault with. Once your list is compiled, check it carefully; do not be surprised if some of those very things that people are upset with are what God himself initiated. What I call 'when God plays hard to get' in this book comes into play. Let us also keep in mind what Jonathan Edwards taught us, that the task of every generation is to discover in which direction the Sovereign Redeemer is moving, then move in that direction. Edwards himself wrote about the surprising work of God in New England in his own day, and we pray for the equivalent – or greater – in our day. But be ready for things that you may find revolting. I'm sorry, but that too is the way it is.

God has been doing this since the Fall of man in the Garden of Eden. In order to establish the forgiveness of sins through the sacrifice of blood, God first did it when he provided Adam and Eve with 'garments of skin' to clothe them after their sin. They tried to cover their nakedness and shame by sewing fig leaves together but God instituted his carefully thought out plan for demanding substitution and satisfaction via the sacrifice of blood in order to appease his wrath and justice (Gen. 3:7,21). The notion of salvation through atonement by the substitutionary death of another has probably been the most repulsive thing about the gospel of God. The popular

Presbyterian minister Harry Emerson Fosdick (1878–1969) wrote that he certainly did not believe in this teaching, neither did he know any 'intelligent' minister who did.

The Fall of Adam and Eve did not take God by surprise. Jesus was regarded in the New Testament as the lamb slain from the foundation of the world (1 Pet. 1:19–20; Rev. 13:8). Therefore the indication of his desire to forgive Adam and Eve was providing them with an atoning sacrifice for their sin in the Garden of Eden. Will we see Adam and Eve in heaven? Yes.

The scarlet thread of redemption continued in God's preference for Abel's offering over Cain's. Abel brought forth 'fat portions from some of the firstborn of his flock' whereas Cain offered 'fruits of the soil'. God looked with favour on Abel but not with regard to Cain's offering (Gen. 4:3–5). This sent a signal early on that God will not respect the work of our own hands or what seems good to us – no matter how great our effort – but only that which he approves of; namely, the blood of a substitute. Charles Haddon Spurgeon used to say that there are two words that need to be in our theological vocabulary: 'substitution' and 'satisfaction'. 'Substitution' refers to one taking our place; 'satisfaction' refers to the blood of the one who took our place which appeases God's justice. All sacrifices of blood in the Old Testament pointed to the ultimate sacrifice of the Lord Jesus Christ.

This still causes many learned and cultured people to say 'Yuk'. The idea of a need for blood sacrifice has been offensive from the time of Cain to this very moment as you hold this book in your hands. Today's sophisticated generation dismisses the idea of a God who demands a substitute for us or requires satisfaction by the shedding of blood. This notion goes back to a pre-scientific age, many say. Wrong. God always has looked for what will offend sophisticated people, possibly because he wants to put obstacles in our way to see if we will believe in his Word only. This is because faith – to be faith – is believing God without evidence for that belief. Only God's Word. 'Faith is being sure of what we hope for and certain of what we do not see' (Heb. 11:1).

In other words, that which makes faith *faith* is when you keep trusting what God says although you are not able to prove your point. When people ask, 'Why does God allow evil when he has the power to stop it?', I answer: to make room for faith. We wouldn't need faith if we could supply the answer to the problem of evil. Neither would we need faith if we could make ourselves look good before our accusers – whether they be sophisticated or not.

It isn't fun when respectable, intelligent people roll their eyes heavenward when they see our 'foolish' stubbornness and adherence to God's chosen manifestation of his glory. The crowning blow among the 'hard sayings' of Jesus came when he said, 'Whoever eats my flesh and drinks my blood has eternal life' (John 6:54). Jesus made no attempt to explain himself; he just let people vent their feelings – which they did. A very interesting and fruitful study is tracing the miracles of Jesus and how many times he waited for the Sabbath to arrive in order to offend the religious people of the day (e.g. John 5:9; 9:14).

God's ultimate sacrifice was on Good Friday. We now know that the ancient sacrificial system under the Law pointed to the event of Jesus' crucifixion. But nobody knew it then, not when it was happening. It was God's secret weapon not only to take his people by surprise but also the devil. Satan conspired with Judas Iscariot, Herod, Pontius Pilate, the chief priests and leading Jews to crucify Jesus. But Paul says it was God's hidden wisdom from the beginning of time. 'None of the rulers of this age understood it, for if they had, they would not have crucified the Lord of glory' (1 Cor. 2:8).

Indeed, had you walked into Jerusalem on Good Friday and asked the religious people, 'What is God doing here today?' they would have answered, 'It's Passover and we can hardly wait to celebrate it – if only that wicked thing on the cross outside the gate would hurry up and die.' No one remotely dreamed at the time that God was in Christ reconciling the world to himself by the death of his Son (2 Cor. 5:19). Never forget that Jesus was crucified outside the city of Jerusalem and God has continued to manifest his glory outside the camp. We therefore must be willing to go outside the camp – continually – and bear his reproach (Heb. 13:12–13). Some would even say, 'The further out the better.'

A funny thing happened to me when I preached at the Airport Christian Fellowship for John and Carol Arnott. It was an honour to be asked, it being the second anniversary of the so-called 'Toronto blessing'. But when I got up to speak, using a text and sermon I knew backwards and forwards – Hebrews 4:16 – I could not preach it. I mean, I could not speak. I was literally kept from uttering two sentences intelligibly together. If you had paid me one million dollars tax free to preach my sermon on Hebrews 4:16 I could not have done it. After some fifteen minutes of intense and embarrassing struggle in trying to preach it I felt an impulse that I should turn to Hebrews 13:13 – not realising what it said: 'Let us, then, go to him outside the camp, bearing the disgrace he bore.' I knew in a split second I was to give up trying to preach on Hebrews 4:16 and preach on Hebrews 13:13. Whereas up to then four thousand people were laughing their heads off, things got amazingly quiet. For the next twenty minutes I preached on Hebrews 13:13 with considerable liberty. Hundreds flocked to the front for prayer, including many ministers. It was an unforgettable night.

But my main point for bringing this up is this: that was the first sermon preached in the Toronto Christian Fellowship. Before then it was the Airport Vineyard Fellowship. The church had been sadly cut off and disenfranchised by the Vineyard hierarchy and on the very day I spoke it took its new name. They were thrust outside the camp. The sermon the Holy Spirit wanted was most appropriate. We must always be prepared to go outside the camp. It isn't fun. But it's good.

The yuk factor can now be defined. It is God's chosen stumbling-block by which he intentionally puts off religious men and women. If he can come up with an event, activity, teaching or manifestation by which 'intelligent' and smug people will conclude, 'This could not possibly be God at work', he says to himself, 'This will do nicely.' 'But we preach Christ crucified; a stumbling-block to Jews and foolishness to Gentiles' (1 Cor. 1:23).

God's own people – his very elect – often initially underestimate the surprising time and way the Holy Spirit enters the scene. In a most insignificant and innocuous place, where he lay down to sleep, using a stone for a pillow, Jacob was made to admit, 'Surely the LORD is in this place, and I was not aware of it' (Gen. 28:16). Speaking personally, almost every pivotal decision I had to make during my twenty-five years at Westminster Chapel was the outcome of having to overcome an initial negative reaction to what I encountered. It isn't fun to climb down – it is so embarrassing. But I had to do it more than once. I was never sorry.

Spirituality could be defined as closing the time gap between God's actual appearing and our acknowledgment of his presence. In other words, how long does it take for you to admit that that was God after all? It took years for some to concede it was God at work in New England between 1735 and 1750 – now known as the Great Awakening. It took a good while before some people in Britain regarded the Welsh Revival as a genuine work of the Spirit and not emotionalism. I think of the British couple who sailed all the way from India to Southampton because they heard that true revival had broken out in Wales. But old friends – Christians – warned them that it was 'only Welsh emotionalism'. The couple never went to Wales but returned to India. Sophisticated religious people have often stopped sincere Christians from embracing what is of God because it is so often tainted with what is undignified and not very traditional.

When Arthur Blessitt began witnessing in Sunset Strip in Hollywood, religious people said 'That can't be God.' But it was. When he erected that large cross and hung it on a wall in what Arthur called His Place, people said, 'That can't be God.' But it was. When he claimed that the Lord told him to take the cross down from the wall and carry it on foot around the world, people said, 'That can't be God.' But it was. When I managed to get Arthur to speak at Westminster Chapel and stay for six weeks, religious people said, 'That can't be God.'

But it was. The best decision I made in twenty-five years at the Chapel was to bring Arthur Blessitt to my old church.

So how long do you suppose it takes you to recognise God's presence? For some it takes years. For some it takes months. For some it takes moments. The degree to which we are familiar with God's own peculiar ways will likely determine how long we take to trace the rainbow through the rain.

When Charlie Colchester, the former churchwarden at Holy Trinity, Brompton, said to Lyndon Bowring and me in a Chinese restaurant in London's Soho, 'Have your guys heard about this Toronto thing?' – referring to people falling on the floor and laughing – I wanted to say 'Yuk'. If you could have put me under a lie detector and asked whether I believed that what Charlie described that night was of God, I would have said 'No' and passed with flying colours. For one thing, I didn't want it to be of God. I find that sort of thing offensive. Furthermore, I didn't want it to be of God because, if it really were, it would have come to Westminster Chapel first! *We* were the ones (I really thought this) who bore the heat of the day, witnessing in the streets of Victoria, praying for the manifestation of God's glory and putting our reputation on the line. So if God were going to do anything in London it would have started with us!

I was wrong. For what was happening in those days at Holy Trinity, Brompton (called the 'Toronto blessing' by the *Sunday Telegraph*) I later came to see really was of God. It was hard to have to admit that. It wasn't easy to face my congregation, having previously publicly stated that it was not of God, and climb down. Some disagreed with me then and some still disagree. Some still continue to say 'Yuk' as I initially did.

Let me gently say that if your own reaction to what is happening in a church, even if it is strange and contrary to tradition, is to say 'Yuk' – or if you find yourself outside your comfort zone – please consider that there is a real possibility that God is behind the whole thing and that he takes responsibility for what you are uneasy with. You would not, would you, consciously want to be against what he is in? Since there is a pattern both in ancient Israel and in church history for God taking the blame for what was at first not appreciated, we must continually be open to the Lord and not be too hasty in dismissing what makes us feel uncomfortable.

As I will take pains to show below, not all that makes us think 'Yuk' is of the Holy Spirit – far from it! But it could be the Holy Spirit and a pattern in church history shows it often is him at work.

I have, I hope, learned to be patient with people whose initial reaction is negative to the new and different (and strange). I've been there and continue to struggle with those whose style and emphasis is quite the opposite to my taste. I therefore do not want this book to be a recipe for how to be strange and please God. And I certainly don't want to be condemnatory. I only want you not to miss what God is up to and be deprived of blessing that you will be so thankful for later on. I am grateful to God for his patience with me and not taking me seriously when I have reacted negatively to what I later came to accept as being from him.

In my book *In Pursuit of His Glory* I tell how I introduced our close friends Randy and Nancy Wall to the ministry of Rodney Howard-Browne. In a word: Rodney and Adonica Howard-Browne visited us in Key Largo and came to the Walls' home (where we were staying) for hamburgers. Rodney prayed for Randy who was immediately touched and overcome by the Spirit. Although he had no background to prepare him for what was coming (the church he attended did not even believe in the gifts of the Spirit), he began laughing uproariously for the next two hours. But his wife Nancy was not amused. 'I am uncomfortable with this', she let us know.

It was not for another year or more that Nancy herself was blessed by the immediate and direct testimony of the Spirit. Her own manifestation of the Spirit was even more bizarre than laughing for hours. She was left with an urge to utter 'Ho!' involuntarily – whether at home, church or in a public restaurant. Yuk! Nancy was embarrassed by this at times, as we can understand. She is a cultured, sophisticated and middle-class church member. This sort of thing had not been in her church background or upbringing – ever. So one day she asked me, 'R.T., why does this urge to shout "Ho!" come to me? Should I not repress it rather than embarrass myself and my friends?'

I replied, 'Nancy, I think God does this to you to see whether you want the anointing of the Spirit more than anything else in the world. He has given you this stigma to see whether you are willing to bear it for the sake of his presence.'

She immediately cried out, 'Ho! Ho! Ho!'

It was outside and I was a little embarrassed. And then I said, 'If you repress this – which you can do anytime you like – this will stop and probably never come back. And you will never forgive yourself and regret it as long as you live.'

But Randy and Nancy began to feel uneasy in the church of which they had been pillars for over twenty years. I felt guilty, having introduced them to a dimension of the Spirit but also a stigma that, for some reason, came alongside at the same time. They eventually found another church where they are welcome. Though this has been an upheaval in their lives they keep saying to me that they cannot thank me enough, that they would not go back to where they were for anything in the world.

If you ask, 'R.T., do you ever "Ho!" or do anything strange?' I answer, 'Not yet'. But the stigma for me has been different. It is more a case of having doors closed where I used to be accepted, noticing that old friends distance themselves from me and having to hear of things put in print that are unflattering and hurtful. But I too would not turn back for anything. I can state categorically that the increase of anointing more than compensates for any measure of loneliness or rejection. There is no substitute for the ungrieved presence of the Holy Spirit. It is just that he accompanies himself so often with an offence to test us whether he means more to us than the approval of friends. He is a jealous God.

I would have to admit that I have had more preparation than some when it comes to being open to the offensive ways of the Holy Spirit. My training for the position I have adopted as a way of life began many years ago. It certainly started when I was a child in my old church in Ashland, Kentucky. I can remember my mother literally running from one side of the church to the other during a service. I was six years old and embarrassed even then. I slipped outside the church. 'What are you doing here, R.T.?' said one to me.

'I don't like the noise', I replied. After we got home I said to my mother, 'Why did you do that?'

She replied, 'Because I was so happy.'

But I was hardly prepared for an advanced course in the surprising and unusual ways of the Spirit that came in the early months of 1956. My 'Damascus Road' experience on 31 October 1955 had catapulted me into a new theological grasp of truth – the belief in election, predestination and the eternal security of the believer. I came to this on my own – with no help from Nazarenes, the people of my old denomination. I thought I had a unique understanding of truth at first, that possibly nobody since the apostle Paul believed what I came to see just by reading the Bible and from what I sensed directly from the Holy Spirit. This continued until I found a group of Baptists in Ashland, led by Pastor Henry Mahan, who accepted me and helped refine and clarify my 'new' theology. It turned out that it wasn't new at all but rather historic Christianity. I am still amazed that God would do this for me. The 'Damascus Road' experience was in fact my baptism in the Spirit. However, my theology is not what I want to talk about in this chapter.

A church service in which I was not present in my old church in Ashland, Kentucky, in April 1956 changed my entire life. It turned my world upside down. Dr Billy Ball, to whom I will refer below, says it was the defining moment of his life as well. This service, perhaps more than any other (including those where I was present) did not shape my theology as such but it helped me to understand how the presence of the Holy Spirit in power can be anything but nice.

I was then a student at Trevecca Nazarene College in Nashville, Tennessee but also the pastor (travelling on weekends) of a small church in Palmer, about a two-hour drive from

Nashville. What I shall describe was considered unusual, if not strange, even then when Nazarenes were less sophisticated. The pastor of the church had planned to hold nightly services but fell ill and asked his associate, Billy Ball, to conduct the meetings and do the preaching. My father wrote me a letter to tell me this but mainly to report 'how wonderful Brother Ball was preaching' and said, 'Son, he has been preaching with more power than I have witnessed since I was a boy.' Dad wrote this to encourage me because he knew how much I enjoyed spending time with Billy Ball in those days. Billy had become my mentor in many ways.

My father's letter, however, did not greatly surprise me. The letter came two months after Billy himself told me what would happen in the Nazarene church in Ashland very soon. It was almost certainly my first exposure to the ministry of the prophetic. He told me in February 1956 that:

1   the senior pastor would shortly become ill;
2   the pastor would ask Billy to do the preaching;
3   Billy would be given unusual power; but
4   something would happen that would thrust him right out of his church!

I remember when he told me this, at his home in Ashland, and how a most unusual but sweet presence of the Holy Spirit fell in the room. It was as though there was a glow in the centre of the room. I also remember believing in my heart that I myself would one day be in an international ministry but could not imagine how that would happen. Nazarenes were very provincial and I always saw myself as a Nazarene forever – no matter what. Therefore I wondered how I could be involved in a worldwide ministry.

What happened was this. The pastor announced that he himself would preach in a series of nightly meetings in April 1956. A worship leader, known then as a song evangelist, was brought in to lead the singing. But a few days before the meeting was to begin Billy received a phone call to see the pastor. I remember Billy saying to me, 'The only thing that troubles me is that in my vision the pastor was in bed in a room that I did not recognise but neither was it a hospital room, so I don't know how this will happen.' But when he arrived at the parsonage in answer to the pastor's wife's phone call she directed him upstairs and said, 'Oh, he is in the room to the right as you come to the top of the stairs, not our regular bedroom.' When Billy entered the room it was exactly as he had seen it in a vision.

The pastor asked Billy to preach in the services. Billy did so and preached night after night with unusual power. That is when my father wrote the letter to me. The thrust of Billy's preaching for four nights was based largely on two verses:

How can ye believe, which receive honour one of another, and seek not the honour that cometh from God only? (John 5:44, AV)

And he said unto them, Ye are they which justify yourselves before men; but God knoweth your hearts: for that which is highly esteemed among men is abomination in the sight of God. (Luke 16:15, AV)

But the pastor showed up on the Thursday evening and said he would preach from now on. This decision would have pleased everybody since the pastor was regarded as one of the greatest preachers of the denomination. But people noticed a difference in the atmosphere. The pastor, though greatly loved and respected by all the people, did not seem to have his usual power in his preaching, certainly nothing like what the growing congregations had witnessed when Billy did the preaching that week.

Three men, members of the church – Ed, Jack and Howard – approached Billy to see if he would join them for a time of prayer. The four men began to pray on that same Thursday evening after people went home from church. They ended up praying for almost the entire night. I later talked with some of these men and asked them what it was like. I wanted to know because the fall-out of this prayer meeting would have a major effect on my own life. Two of them said they felt a burden for one man in particular but did not discuss it with each other; it turned out to be the same person each felt led to pray for. One of the men told me he had a vision of hell – or what he assumed must be hell. He said he saw only faces, or heads, of people floating in what looked like burning sulphur. Their faces were contorted and in despair. He recognised them as people he knew and was shocked since they were regarded as strong members of the church. The four men did not talk with each other during the night but prayed until about five o'clock in the morning. They returned to their homes in order to go to work that day. Billy assumed he would not be asked to preach on the Friday evening since the pastor had returned to the pulpit the evening before. But he was asked during the day to conduct the Friday evening service and preach.

The four men met at church at seven o'clock on Friday evening to spend more time in prayer. The service began at seven-thirty with congregational singing. Billy left the three men in the room in which they were praying and took his seat on the platform. During the congregational singing the three other men burst into the service and began to exhort the people. Two of the men took their seats after a few minutes, but Ed kept it up – walking up and down the centre aisle of the church 'like a wild man', according to my dad. The singing came to a halt while Ed addressed the shocked congregation. The organist, who happened to be my Aunt Ruth, began to play with the hope that Ed would take the hint and sit down. But he didn't. He even told Aunt Ruth to stop playing. She did. Ed continued to speak to the people, shouting with all his might. My dad, who witnessed the whole episode, bowed his head and prayed that Ed would please stop this ranting and raving.

But he didn't. As for my father, he was quite out of his comfort zone. Ed continued, urging the people to repent. He then began to say that someone present was seriously grieving the Holy Spirit, that this person was holding back what could be great revival. Different ones present later told me they thought it could be them – as if to say in their hearts, 'Is it I?' Ed kept exhorting the congregation of about 400 for nearly thirty minutes and then stated that 'Ichabod' was written over the door of the church. The Holy Spirit was being quenched. The pastor, who had asked Billy to take the service, unexpectedly turned up and took his seat on the platform.

Ed did not see him but continued, 'I see a coffin, the person in it is holding up the revival. I know this man. I love this man. I love him very much. I know his address. I fear for this man.'

My dad continued to plead with the Lord that this would end. Whereas some sensed great fear and personal conviction, my father and grandmother, who was also present, only wanted Ed to stop his unreasonable if not irrational behaviour. At some point during Ed's shouting to the people a haze settled on the service. Not all saw it. My dad didn't see it. Ed saw it but thought that something had gone wrong with his eyes since he could not see past the haze. He kept rubbing his eyes to see better and had no idea what it was or what it meant.

The song evangelist decided to stand in the pulpit and ask the people to sing a well-known song called 'The unclouded day'. At this point Billy walked to the pulpit and motioned for the song leader not to proceed since Billy wanted to say something. My dad was greatly relieved to see Billy take charge because it was assumed Billy would bring a sense of sanity and order to the service that had become completely out of control. The service was almost like a nightmare to some. But all were pleased that Billy would take over.

'This is the greatest demonstration of the Holy Ghost I have ever seen', Billy said. My dad said to himself, 'Oh no, Brother Ball is condoning this wild fanaticism.' But Billy began reading aloud the account of Ananias who lied to the Holy Spirit. He read the first five verses of Acts 5 and sat down. A number of people got out of their seats and came to the altar. Six or seven were reportedly converted or, at least, got spiritual help. At this point the pastor took charge and asked if anybody else wanted to come forward for prayer, then dismissed the service.

There were mixed reactions to the service, which turned out to be historic in many ways. Some felt a great conviction of sin and feared they were the person Ed had in mind. From all accounts it was no time for laughter but a great sense of fear and sobriety. One old lady, highly respected for her godliness, said, 'I thought the days of Holy Ghost manifestations like this were over but this is the best I have seen.' Others, however, were horrified and upset that such an undignified service was allowed to continue. No one thought it was very nice.

On the Saturday evening the pastor was feeling better and did the preaching. After the service he asked to meet with the four men – Howard, Ed, Jack and Billy Ball – and said to them, 'Who are you men after?' They were taken aback by the question and did not know how to answer. They all said, 'We are not after anybody.' Then the pastor focused on Ed, 'Who are you after?' Ed replied he was after no one but admitted that he had a burden to pray for him, that is, the pastor who was questioning them. The pastor then asked Ed, 'Who did you have in mind last night when you exhorted the people like you did?' Edward replied that it was the pastor himself he had in mind on the Friday night.

The pastor then turned to each of them to see if they agreed with Ed, asking Billy first. Billy said that he had a burden to pray for the pastor during the all-night prayer meeting that began Thursday evening but had not said this to a single soul. Each man then said that they felt in their hearts that Ed had the pastor in mind during the Friday service but none of them discussed this among themselves. This very moment, then, when the pastor called the four men for this meeting, was the first time they actually spoke to each other on the subject.

At this point the pastor asked them, 'What have I done? What sin have I committed?' No one knew what to say in reply. The pastor then knelt at the altar – they thought he did so mockingly – and said, 'I am the penitent, now you men pray for me.' The men felt helpless and were not able to pray at all. They did not believe the pastor was really sincere. But they did their best to pray but felt no liberty in doing so. After an hour or so they all dispersed and went to their homes.

The next morning, Sunday, the pastor phoned each of the members of his board. My dad was on the board and told me verbatim what happened. 'I now know who the men had in mind Friday night', he said to my father.

'Who?' my father anxiously asked.

'Me.'

'No, it can't be you, surely not.'

'Yes, I am the man.'

My father was disgusted with the four men, including Billy Ball. How dare they question the pastor, Dad thought. This pastor was not only regarded as one of the greatest preachers of the denomination but also as very humble and godly.

Within forty-eight hours Billy Ball was dismissed as the associate pastor of the Nazarene church and immediately had to find a place to live and get any kind of a job.

It will be recalled that I was not present at this service. But I received a letter from my father a few days later. Whereas the previous letter from my father sang Billy Ball's praises, this letter said: 'Son, have nothing to do with Billy Ball. Do not write him, do not call him. Something terrible has happened in our church. Billy Ball has been asked to leave and resign as associate pastor. Nothing immoral. But have nothing to do with him.'

I was puzzled. Sobered. As I drove in my car after reading the letter I had a clear witness of the Holy Spirit – as clear as an audible voice – to turn to Philippians 1:12, not knowing what it would say. Nothing like this had happened to me before. I stopped the car, opened my Bible to read it: 'But I would ye should understand, brethren, that the things which happened unto me have fallen out rather unto the furtherance of the gospel' (AV).

I knew at once that it referred to Billy Ball. To me it meant that Billy had not done anything wrong, whatever had happened, but had been led by the Holy Spirit. But it would equally refer to me, as I would see later. For that verse held me more than anything else over the next several years. All this led to the first break with my dad, the most godly and sincere Christian I have ever known. It was the beginning of a long, hard, bleak era in which I would crave vindication more than the world itself.

This then is why the aforementioned service, though I was not present at it, changed my life. Nothing was ever to be the same again. One year before I was given a brand new 1955 Chevrolet by my godly grandmother. She was widely regarded as possibly the most saintly elderly woman in that church. As I said above, she was also present in that extraordinary service. But my standing on the side of Billy Ball, combined with a new theological perspective, changed everything. In a word: she took the car back! I would ask myself in those days, 'How could she do this? Had I broken with God? Had I gone out into the world. Had I fallen into sin?' No. But I broke with her concept of God. It led to her disinheriting me. My dad went through deep grief, even comparing it to what he felt when my mother died three years before.

Who was right? Was the pastor right to phone the key members of the church the Sunday morning after confronting the men? Was the church board right to dismiss Billy Ball? Or do it so soon? Was Billy Ball right to walk to the pulpit, endorse all that had happened and then read Acts 5:1–5? Was Ed right to interrupt the service as he did – and then cry out, 'God has written "Ichabod" over this church'? Was my dad right to order me to break all connections with Billy Ball? Was my grandmother right to take back the car and eventually disinherit me? And was I myself right to stand with Billy Ball and take the view that the service – strange and terrible as it seemed to be – was actually orchestrated by the Holy Spirit? Would God really be in this? If so, how could such godly people miss it?

I return to the matter of the haze. During the Friday service when a haze filled the auditorium, Billy Ball was one who saw it. He has commented to me many times that he never knew such power in all his life as he had in the pulpit as he read from Acts 5:1–5, that it is even difficult to imagine any ancient prophet having more power than he felt as he read those verses. As for Ed, he certainly saw the haze but was confused by it and was afraid to mention it to anybody for weeks lest they say even more critical things to him.

The haze was the *kabodh* (Hebrew), meaning the *shekinah* glory of God. It is what disrupted the priests in their work in the temple. 'Then the temple of the LORD was filled with a cloud, and the priests could not perform their service because of the cloud, for the glory of the LORD filled the temple of God' (2 Chron. 5:13–14; cf. 1 Kgs. 8:10–11). Jack Hayford described this phenomenon in his own testimony, which I heard him give. When he had a small church of about 300 people, he walked into his auditorium one Saturday (with nobody else in it) and saw this haze. 'It's what you think it is', the Lord said to Jack. Then the Lord said to him, 'I will give my glory to dwell in this church.' From that very time his church began to be blessed in ever-increasing measure and became the wonderful church it is today.

But the *kabodh* in that Kentucky church service was not a promise of growth and blessing, quite the opposite. It was instead a seal of the Holy Spirit on that unforgettable service in which people thought such happenings could not possibly be instigated of God. God is surely too nice to do that sort of thing. Although there was a mixed reaction, most concluded that it was not of God. But I believe that it was.

My old church in Ashland continued on for years as if nothing happened. To me it was not unlike the temple in Jerusalem continuing on after Jesus' death on the cross. Though the veil inside the temple was torn from top to bottom, the priests went back to business as usual. There was no outward sign or even hint that God wrote 'Ichabod' over the temple. In much the same way, those who continued to worship at the Ashland church, as far as I know, sensed nothing different. It is like that statement of the Episcopal rector who said, 'If the Holy Spirit were completely withdrawn from the Church today, ninety per cent of the work of the Church would continue as if nothing had happened.' But from that time, slowly but surely, the spirit and power of my old home Nazarene church went down, down, down. Within a generation it had lost its strategic influence and the numbers dwindled to the size of a small church. As for the pastor, he soon lost the support of many who had defended him at the time – even those who were most indignant against Billy and the three other men. He continued on until, a few years later, he died a premature death.

Many people of the Ashland congregation warned me that I would not be used of God for taking this stand. Billy and I would 'eat dust', a number of them said. My father sincerely believed I had got right out of God's will and was bringing judgment on myself, and with tears he continually and lovingly but firmly warned me. By siding with Billy Ball and suggesting that the existing pastor could have seriously quenched and grieved the Holy Spirit, my dad said we had gone against God's anointed and we would pay dearly. In addition to all the above my own radical theological change paralleled all this; I came to embrace the doctrines of sovereign grace and this – certainly to my dad – confirmed all the more that I was utterly in the wrong.

I tried not to let that bother me too much, but it still hurt to be looked upon with disdain. I went through times when I wondered if I had got it wrong after all. At times I even hoped I was wrong, especially after coming to Westminster Chapel. It was easier to dismiss the aforementioned episode as utter fanaticism so I need not fear God would do anything strange in the Chapel, or require me to have to tolerate such strangeness. The person to give me the most objectivity about that service in 1956 was none other than Dr Martyn Lloyd-Jones many years later. On two different occasions, over three years, I repeated the above story, hoping he would look at me and say (as he had done dozens of times on other issues), 'Now look here. This was quite wrong.' Or something like that. But no. Both times he came up with the same thing: God was indeed wanting to do something in that church and the men were led of the Holy Spirit. Dr Lloyd-Jones frequently surprised people by his ability to recognise God at work when no one else could.

In the summer of 1979, some twenty-three years later, my beloved dad visited us in London, approximately two years after I became the minister of Westminster Chapel. I was not prepared for what he unexpectedly said to me. Given my own dad's culture and background I found this quite extraordinary. I heard him utter words I used to long for. I could hardly believe what I was hearing, but he actually said to me: 'I'm sorry, son, I was wrong. God's hand has been on you all these years and I am so proud to have you as a son.' As for Billy Ball, he felt forced to leave his old denomination in 1956 but went from strength to strength in another church. Though Billy and I were not destined to have a ministry together (as I used to suppose), he became the pastor of a church that grew to be the largest church in the state of Ohio. He became one of the most popular and respected preachers in his movement and has been honoured by many thousands from all over the world for his faithfulness to God and his Word.

The question is: are there objective tests by which a person who doesn't want to be deceived and who doesn't want to miss out on God's blessing can be guided? I really do wish I knew the answer to this. I have my own dilemma in this area. For why is it that sincere Christians who are devoted to pleasing God, like my own father, can miss the mark regarding God's will and presence? How could my dad or my godly grandmother be on the wrong side of the issue in those hard days of 1956? Why did not everybody see the haze? Or would they have recognised it for what it was? What were the ingredients in the Ashland service that led Dr Martyn Lloyd-Jones to believe it was of God?

I cannot be sure how I myself would have reacted had I been present. Had not the Holy Spirit given me Philippians 1:12 at a critical time I might well have sided with the majority who felt that Billy Ball and Ed were deceived and governed solely by the flesh. I would never have been friendly with Billy Ball again, neither would I have had him as a mentor.

I had opposed the Toronto blessing until I watched a close friend fall on his face when prayed for in my old vestry. He himself was not by nature open to that sort of thing and had not even heard of the Toronto phenomenon but politely allowed a ministerial friend pray for him. When he went to the floor involuntarily and lay there helplessly for ten minutes, I began to fear I was on the wrong side of that issue. *I cannot think of anything worse than being near where God is at work but missing out on it because of my own prejudice.*

At the end of the day – as to who immediately recognises the Holy Spirit and who doesn't – I think it comes down to the sovereignty of God. There is more than one sphere in which the sovereignty of God works. He is sovereign in salvation; he saves some but (apparently) not all. He is sovereign in healing; he heals some but (apparently) not all. The gifts of the Spirit are meted out as he sovereignly determines (1 Cor. 12:11,18). So too, I must conclude, with the unusual ways God is pleased to show up. He opens the eyes of some and lets the rest say

'Yuk'. But sometimes, thankfully and mercifully, he changes those of us who say 'Yuk' at first and graciously humbles us.

All I know is, we must try not to be hasty in rejecting what isn't very appealing. We may have to eat our words. His ways are higher than our ways. He has chosen the foolish things of the world to confound the wise. As Jesus put it, 'I praise you, Father, Lord of heaven and earth, because you have hidden these things from the wise and learned, and revealed them to little children. Yes, Father, for this was your good pleasure' (Matt. 11:25–26). A further irony – call it God's sense of humour if you like – is that so many of the proponents of the sovereignty of God (who sometimes think they have a franchise on this truth) are sovereignly blinded to the things of the Holy Spirit. I wish it weren't so. They remind me of A.W. Tozer's words, that there is nothing worse than people who don't have the Spirit but who talk a lot about the Spirit as though they did.

Let us pray that God will somehow keep us from grieving his Holy Spirit and graciously let us in on what he is up to. Let us be patient with those who oppose what we accept; for were it not for the grace of God we too would be where they are. I just pray that God won't be so nice to you and me as to leave us in our smugness and pass us by when it comes to knowing his ways.

No, it isn't the greatest fun in the world to be found outside your comfort zone or to bear any kind of stigma. But down the road the reward is worth waiting for.

7

The Sin Jesus Hated Most

'The Pharisee stood up and prayed about himself: 'God, I thank
you that I am not like other men'

Luke 18:11

I had an experience in Jerusalem recently for which I was not
prepared. Some of us, including the former Archbishop of
Canterbury and his wife – Lord and Lady Carey – and Canon
Andrew White of Coventry Cathedral, had a Sabbath meal on a
Friday evening with a prominent Israeli rabbi and his family. It
was a wonderful evening. Rabbi David Rosen, the Jerusalem-
based International Director of Interreligious Affairs of the
American Jewish Committee, endeared himself to all of us as he
demonstrated with his wife and two children what their Sabbath
evenings are like. It even brought us to tears. If most people we
may be tempted to call Pharisees are cold, I have to admit that
this man, a modern self-confessed Pharisee, was very warm.

But what almost startled me prior to my getting to know him – as well as discussing the matter with him – was the complimentary way he had referred to a Pharisee. I was stunned at first because nearly all I have known about a Pharisee is not good, and calling one a Pharisee therefore is not a compliment (to put it mildly). But Rabbi Rosen wants to be seen as a Pharisee in our day and would wear the label as a badge of honour. To make sure I wasn't misunderstanding him I asked him if indeed I rightly discerned this? Absolutely, he replied. He has since sent an informative email on the matter.

You might like to know that he has read this chapter and the one which follows. However, he sees a very important distinction between those Pharisees Jesus is recorded as addressing and Pharisees as they are truly to be understood. He also believes that today's successors in Israel, of which he is one, bear no resemblance to those described in the New Testament. Not only that; he told me that he would feel much the same as I do towards those Pharisees Jesus is recorded as addressing. Rabbi Rosen and I are in continuing dialogue about this. We may even write a book together on it one day!

In the four Gospels, the Pharisees are almost entirely portrayed as the bad guys. And yet I keep in mind that on at least one occasion Jesus accepted an invitation to have dinner with a Pharisee (Luke 11:37). The meal was paralleled by Jesus ruthlessly exposing the hearts of the Pharisees – who he tended to put altogether in one lump – and called them 'You foolish people' (v. 40). The Pharisee might have been a nice man, but Jesus was not very nice to him!

The Pharisees (a word which probably means the 'separated ones') emerged in the second century BC. They were a strict sect made up mostly of ordinary Jews, unlike the Sadducees who were members of the families of priests. Pharisees were far more numerous than Sadducees but not so prestigious. The Pharisees kept closely to the Mosaic Law and often embellished the Law with countless rules so that these rules were very hard to keep. They saw themselves as a cut above everybody else. They counted work on the Sabbath as walking more than a kilometre from one's town, carrying any kind of load or lighting a fire in the home. It led to people being concerned to keep the Law in every detail. The Pharisees believed that their rules built a 'fence around the Law' so that by keeping these rules people would be in less danger of disobeying the actual Law of God.

One must not forget that many of them were no doubt pious men. Some scholars reckon that when Jesus described the Pharisee in the parable in Luke 18:9–14, some Pharisees really did do such things as he boasted of – fasting twice a week and giving a tenth of all they earn, not to mention the fact that they would never be guilty of wrong doing such as robbing or committing adultery. They were regarded as the truly righteous people of their day. They were without question the backbone of their synagogues and would in some cases be like certain Evangelicals today who carry their big black Bibles to church and would never smoke or touch a drop of alcohol or watch a movie that was anything but for the whole family. But they tended to look down on those who did not keep their rules and called such people 'sinners'. Remember too that Nicodemus, who was a secret follower of Jesus, was a Pharisee. So was the apostle Paul before he was converted.

Dr Martyn Lloyd-Jones used to relish telling the story

(which I have in print elsewhere but which is too good not to mention here) of two unforgettable weeks he and Mrs Lloyd-Jones spent in America many years ago. The first week was with a very religious couple in White Sulphur Springs, West Virginia, who were the quintessence of American fundamentalism. This man and his wife were disgusted at 'so-called' Christians who smoke and drink and, according to Dr Lloyd-Jones, it seemed he could never get through a meal in the entire first week without referring in disdain to 'these people who call themselves Christians' who smoke or use alcohol. For one thing, he said, it is 'blowing away money' and wasting God's money. Dr Lloyd-Jones looked across the table and asked the lady, who dressed very fashionably, how much her dress cost? Things got very quiet. It was ridiculously expensive. But when the week was over, even though they enjoyed much of it, the Lloyd-Joneses were rather relieved to get away from them.

But there is more. Their next stop was in Grand Rapids, Michigan, where they were to spend a week. They were amused to note that the man who fetched them at the airport was smoking a big cigar, and when they got to his house he said, 'Doctor, would you like a whiskey?' Both Dr and Mrs Lloyd-Jones were intrigued at the contrast between the two couples. Dr Lloyd-Jones stressed that both couples, though very different, equally loved the Lord.

But that is not the end of the story. On the Sunday night after the church service in which Dr Lloyd-Jones preached, he noticed a Howard Johnson's restaurant and said, 'Oh look, there is a Howard Johnson's. I love their ice cream. Do you suppose we could stop and have some?' Things went quiet. But the host politely pulled over and went into the parking lot. As they sat at the table Dr Lloyd-Jones noticed that all were quiet. He spoke up, 'Is anything wrong?'

'No, of course not', the man replied.

'Now look here', said Dr Lloyd-Jones, 'We have been together these days and something is clearly wrong. Please tell me what it is.'

The man finally agreed. 'The problem is, Dr Lloyd-Jones, today is the Sabbath and we do not buy anything on the Sabbath.'

When they returned to their room, Dr Lloyd-Jones said to his wife, 'It seems everybody has to have something they are against so they can feel a bit righteous – I wonder what it is with us? There must be something!'

Whatever, this is often true with so many of us; it seems there are one or two areas, at least, in which we have strong views about something. These views may unconsciously make us think they compensate for other liberties we allow for ourselves (if not too many know about them!). An Episcopalian joke in America is: what is the difference between Southern Baptists and Episcopalians? Answer: the Episcopalians speak to each other in the wine store. I have seen it a thousand times, the best of people who have their secret 'sins' – even if they are not really sins but controversial practices they allow. Equally they have one or two strong views about this or that which gives them a feeling they haven't gone completely off the rails.

It is said that when the German Christians saw the American believers with all their gold and diamonds they were so shocked they dropped their cigars into their beer! I am also reminded of the story of when the great Charles Spurgeon, who loved a cigar, met the famous D.L. Moody. Moody rebuked Spurgeon for smoking. Spurgeon replied that there was not one word in the Bible about 'this', referring to his cigar, but that there was a lot in the Bible about 'that', gently poking Moody in his extended stomach. Let no one think I am happy about cigars! However, the problem is that issues such as smoking and drinking become like the Pharisees' 'rules', which you had to keep or be looked down on.

But given the fact that Pharisees were pious, faithful and the stalwarts of the synagogues in ancient Judaism, why was Jesus so hard on them? Should he not have congratulated them, as if to say, 'You are greatly needed here in Jerusalem these days. I can't imagine what things would be like were it not for you.' No. He never congratulated them once or gave the slightest hint they were either needed or appreciated. He was harsh and rugged with them. Why? The answer to this question, which will come clearer as we proceed, is why the present chapter is so important to this book.

What is most interesting to me is that Jesus was patient, loving and gracious to the woman caught in the sin of adultery, unlike the Pharisees who were chuffed (but supposedly indignant) that they found this woman in the act of sin (John 8:1–11). Jesus did not ever appear to show tender feelings toward the Pharisees. He was not nice to them, despite the fact that they upheld the infallibility of the Bible, believed in resurrected life beyond the grave (unlike the Sadducees) and adhered to a number of practices which Jesus also affirmed.

When I was a young Christian I used to wonder why so much attention was given in the four Gospels to the Pharisees since they do not exist today. Was this not a waste of space?

Why should we have to read about irrelevant people? I have since learned of course that Pharisees do indeed exist today. And I fear I am one of them in too many ways. But other reasons we must listen to what Jesus said to them and about them is because:

1 his words were infallible;
2 his judgment perfectly mirrored the will of the Father (John 5:19); and
3 we too would be the objects of Jesus' firm words to the degree we too are Pharisees.

We are not exempt. His ruthless exposure of the ways of the Pharisees bears our attention. If Jesus was angry with them – then – so would the Father feel the same way about us – now.

What Jesus therefore said to the Pharisees – and about them – must be taken seriously and applied to our lives today. I for one do not want to be a Pharisee. Do you think there is a possibility you could be a Pharisee? To the degree I am one I should be most uncomfortable. If Jesus was not nice to the ancient Pharisees I should be very worried indeed if he is nice to me when I am very like them.

The Pharisees' Comfort Zone

Their traditions
Their extra-biblical rules became a tradition that you were required to keep or you did not love God or respect the Law. Some Pharisees came up to Galilee all the way from Jerusalem just to ask Jesus, 'Why do your disciples break the tradition of

the elders? They don't wash their hands before they eat!' (Matt. 15:1–2). Imagine being so threatened by Jesus that one walks for three days just to see why he did not keep certain rules! This washing of hands was not merely a health matter, by the way, it was a ritualistic thing you did that showed you adhered to the 'party line'.

Is tradition important to you? Tradition was very important to the Pharisees. This doesn't make you a Pharisee. There is nothing particularly wrong with tradition. Sometimes it is quite valuable. The problem is, we end up equating it with the Word of God and, if we are not careful, find it difficult to separate the two – thus making tradition idolatrous.

Some good people do this with the Schofield Bible. This popular Bible has notes that accompany the Word of God which have unwittingly led many Christians, perhaps more so in America, not to know the difference between Schofield's own comments (some of which are good) and the unedited Word (which alone is infallible). I have had people heatedly quote 'Scripture' to me from a Schofield Bible, only to discover they were reading what Schofield said in the margins or at the bottom of each page. My point is this: when Scripture and commentaries on Scripture are put alongside each other with equal authority so that one is to be revered as much as the other, it is idolatry. That is what the Pharisees did with their rules that turned into traditions which turned into Law.

I used to say that England is the most traditional country in the world and Westminster Chapel was the most traditional church in England. Sandy Millar lovingly said to me that we were 'back in the sixties', meaning that our style resonates with the way churches were in the 1960s. I took him seriously, tried to make some changes, and have been grateful for a friend who would speak like that to me. And this was near the end of my time there! For I too am comfortable with leaving things be lest we rock the boat and cause trouble.

How they found significance

Any psychologist, including a Christian psychologist, will tell you that we were made to feel significant. Dale Carnegie, author of *How to Win Friends and Influence People*, says that the strongest urge in the human race is the desire to feel important. We were made this way. A person who does not find significance will end up with all sorts of problems, including severe emotional problems.

The question is: how do we find significance? The answer is: in God. If we don't find our significance in God, namely in his Son Jesus Christ, we will be pursuing unjust goals – the problem with God's ancient people. 'I was enraged by his *sinful greed*', a Hebrew word, as we saw in Chapter 5, that essentially means 'unjust goals' (Isa. 57:17). I have done this so many times I blush to think about it.

And that was a great deal of the reason for the Pharisees' problems. Mind you, they did not think there was a problem in the first place. But there were very serious problems indeed and one of them was that they sought to achieve significance in being admired. 'They loved to be greeted in the market-places and to have men call them "Rabbi" ' (Matt. 23:7). They 'loved the praise from men more than praise from God' (John 12:43). That was the essence of their comfort zone: being applauded, being complimented, being respected and being openly referred to. Do that and you had no problem with them. Jesus didn't do that and had problems with them. These pious men were right in the middle of the conspiracy to have Jesus crucified (John 11:45–47).

Is it not amazing to discover how some people who on the surface seem so godly can become so mean when you cross them? Religious people are the meanest people in the world. Let them remain undisturbed in their comfort zones and they are as sweet as the godfather of the Mafia with his grandchildren. But cross them? Oh dear.

They further sought significance like this: they compared themselves with others – always people they could safely label 'sinners'. That way they always came out on top. So in the aforementioned parable the Pharisee boasted of his good works, then added: 'God, I thank you that I am not like other men – robbers, evildoers, adulterers – or even like this tax collector' (Luke 18:11). We can all find someone who is less righteous than we are to whom we can compare ourselves and we therefore come forth smelling like a rose. 'Comparisons are odious', said Shakespeare, referring to comparing one person against another; but it is perhaps even more odious when we do this to make ourselves look good. 'At least I'm not as bad as so-and-so.'

The Pharisees even did this when it came to the sainted dead. They piously lamented that the great men of God of the past – prophets, for example – were not appreciated in their own day, some were even persecuted. They would lead the way in extolling the virtues of these great people of yore and proved it by building tombs for them and decorating their graves. Who else was doing this? No one. 'No one else cares', said the Pharisees. 'But we do. We will even have annual conferences and learned lectures that show today's generation what really ought to be happening.' Moreover, 'If we had lived in the days of our forefathers, we would not have taken part with them in shedding the blood of the prophets' (Matt. 23:30). In a word: they believed they were not only a cut above today's professing believers, they were even better than anyone else in previous generations. This way they found significance.

They even got their sense of significance in the way they dressed. 'Oh yes', said Jesus. 'Everything they do is done for men to see: They make their phylacteries wide and the tassels on their garments long' (Matt. 23:5). Dress is very important to a Pharisee; always has been, always will be. They will not be the slightest bit convicted over holding a grudge or speaking evil of fellow believers, but they go to pains to look good. To look nice. More than nice. So people will say, 'I love that suit. I love that dress. I love your hair.'

Louise and I will never forget attending the large Baptist convention in Dallas, Texas, in 1985. By then both of us had become very proper and British and were not prepared for the advice a dear friend gave Louise. 'Bring at least two sets of clothes for each day. And you might want to bring different colours of nail polish to go with the various outfits. Most of the women take that little bit of extra time to co-ordinate their colours that way.'

My district superintendent in my old denomination was known for his 'radical preaching'. He preached against women wearing make-up, sleeveless blouses and their wearing short hairstyles. In one camp meeting he was one of two preachers; the other was a Scot (who deeply impacted me) who reportedly came with ten sermons and one suit. They said my old district superintendent came to that camp meeting to preach with ten suits and one sermon. I used to admire him. This was before he died a few years later living with another man's wife. Jesus called it straining out a gnat and swallowing a camel (Matt. 23:24). Perhaps not your typical Pharisee because I would like to think that most people who had legalistic tendencies were at least moral men and women. But the funny thing is, this particular man is the very one who told my dad I would 'eat dust' because I stood with Billy Ball back in 1956.

The Pharisees had a serious problem when it came to money. When Jesus spoke about money (the case can be made he had more to say about this than anything else), the Pharisees became uncomfortable. When he said we cannot serve two masters, either we will hate the one and love the other or be devoted to the one and despise the other because we 'cannot serve both God and Money', the Pharisees 'sneered' at Jesus. And Luke tells us why: they 'loved money' (Luke 16:14). The Authorised Version translates *philargurus* as 'covetous'. Virtually the same word is used in 1 Timothy 6:10 when Paul said that the 'love of money is a root of all evil'. The point is, the Pharisees were motivated by the love of money.

We are talking about the chief enemies of Jesus – who saw right through them – who found their significance in what people said positively about them, by comparing themselves with others and by their very appearance. I wonder how many preachers today need the good suit or clerical garb just to look successful in order to feel important and significant. If I am not careful I will end up a Pharisee in judging them, but I only know so many give the impression, even if unintentionally, that their appearance is an essential ingredient to their sense of significance.

Motivation

How do you persuade a Pharisee to give to the poor? The answer is very simple: hire a couple of trumpeters – a band would be better – and get everyone's attention with the music. They announced their giving by the sound of trumpets in the synagogues and on the streets for one reason: 'to be seen of men'. And how do you suppose you get a Pharisee to pray? Jesus said, 'They love to pray'. If Jesus had said only that they love to pray he would have complimented them. I love to pray. Do you love to pray? Nothing wrong with loving to pray. For that's good. But with the Pharisees, 'They love to pray standing in the synagogues and on the street corners to be seen by men.' The way you get them to stop praying is to walk away while they are doing it. For there is no motivation left if no one is noticing.

And since we know that Pharisees fasted twice a week, what do you suppose lay behind that worthy practice? They made sure you saw them. First, they looked sombre (possibly not too hard for some Pharisees anyway). Second, they disfigured their faces – they put on a facial expression that told you they were carrying heavy-duty burdens; this was important stuff, mind you. They didn't even comb their hair (they were afraid you wouldn't otherwise notice) when they skipped a meal or two. Read it all in Matthew 5:1–18.

In a word: they were starving for recognition. As long as they got credit for giving, praying or fasting, you could count on them – every time. Take away the credit, the tax exemption, the plaque on the wall, the public knowledge of a generous donation, the thanks before all for doing the flowers in front of the pulpit or for washing up in the church kitchen, then there aren't many in the queue wanting to help. Pharisees don't particularly enjoy working behind the scenes, driving someone to church when nobody knows about it, visiting the sick without telling it or giving until their pockets are empty and only God taking notice.

A lady came up to Louise and me in Fort Lauderdale once to say she had been visiting those who were housebound all week.

'Wonderful', I said. 'This is great.'

She said she got so much joy in doing this.

'I believe you', we replied.

And then she said (with a straight face), 'The greatest joy is in not telling it.'

The problem with Pharisees was they so often had no objectivity about themselves. This is because their main problem was that they had no sense of sin. None. Sin to them was always in what you do or don't do. Not what you think or feel. It was all outward appearance. They forgot that God looks on the heart (1 Sam. 16:7).

Priorities

The theological assumptions and priorities of Pharisees can be quickly summed up: their theology was more important than people. They really didn't care about people. It was all theology. Hold to the truth. Contend for the faith. Keep the party line. Above all, remember the Sabbath. Yes. The Sabbath.

'But my word, dear Pharisee, a blind person was healed.'

'Oh yes, but it happened on the Sabbath', comes the terse retort.

'You don't seem to understand, a miracle has taken place. A person who was born blind and has never seen can now see!'

'*But you* don't understand', says the Pharisee with as much warmth as you can find in an igloo. 'Truth is at stake here. Something has gone terribly wrong if a person is healed on the Sabbath. Therefore we cannot rejoice when error is clearly being upheld.'

Read it for yourself in John 9. Not a single person seemed to be blessed that a blind man could now see. All they could think about was theology.

It is almost hilarious that Jesus again and again seemed to wait for the Sabbath before he healed people. Read Matthew 12:2; Mark 2:24; Luke 6:2,6 and Luke 14:3 for a start. You get the picture that he sees a needy person but says to himself, 'It's only two more days until the Sabbath is here and I will wait in order to heal this person then.' In other words, Jesus attacked the Pharisees – not for their upholding the Law but for putting their traditions and party line alongside Holy Scripture as if they were of the same authority. There isn't a single word in the Law that says a person should not be made well on the Sabbath.

Not only did they not care about people, they 'tie up heavy loads and put them on men's shoulders, but they themselves are not willing to life a finger to move them' (Matt. 23:4). They were great at giving orders. They told people what to do. It did not seem to bother them that they could get people around them to do this and that but they themselves did not get their hands dirty. This is why Jesus said, 'They do not practise what they preach' (Matt. 23:3).

How they perpetuated their comfort zone

You may ask, 'How could they do this and not feel any conscience about it? How can they sleep at night?' The answer is what I said above: they had no sense of sin. Sin to them is not what you think, it is what you do. This is why Jesus explained the Law as he did: if you hate, you have already committed murder in your heart; if you lusted after a woman (or caused her to lust), you have committed adultery in your heart (Matt. 5:21, 28). But they could not see it that way. This is why they hated all that Jesus preached and did. He did not hold to the party line. They never saw their own sin – ever, as far as we can tell. This is why Jesus said that it was the tax collector, so looked down on by the Pharisee, who was justified before God rather than the Pharisee. For the tax collector prayed, not even being able to look up to heaven but beat his breast and said, 'God, have mercy on me, a sinner' (Luke 18:13–14).

They further perpetuated their comfort zones by loopholes they somehow found that set them free from the kind of obedience they were uncomfortable with. The fences that they erected that supposedly protected the Law actually served in some cases to give a way out *not* to obey the Law strictly at all! Jesus nailed them to the wall in this area. The commandment to honour both father and mother was undeniable – this being the Fifth Commandment. But they had a way of keeping their parents from receiving money that ought to go to them by a rule that enabled them to divert it to the temple or synagogue instead.

> You [Pharisees] say that if a man says to his father or mother, 'Whatever help you might otherwise have received from me is a gift devoted to God [the money should go to the Lord instead in this case],' he is not to 'honour his father' with it. Thus you nullify the word of God for the sake of your tradition. (Matt. 15:5–6)

When Jesus said that one cannot enter the kingdom of heaven unless one's righteousness actually surpasses that of the Pharisees, nobody could believe their ears. For the ordinary Jew living at the time thought they were so far beneath a Pharisee; the thought of exceeding the righteousness of a Pharisee seemed over the top. But Jesus knew exactly what he was talking about; not only are we justified by faith in Jesus who perfectly fulfilled the Law on our behalf but our very righteousness, when we follow Jesus, far outdistances that of the Pharisee. For the Pharisee never felt any conscience about speaking evil of another, hurting their reputation, holding a grudge or not forgiving an enemy.

Jesus knew this. He knew that talk about sin in the heart is what they loathed and despised. It is not what *enters* a person's mouth that makes them unclean; it is what *comes out* of it. It is not what enters the stomach and goes out of the body that defiles a person; it is what comes from the heart which makes them 'unclean'. 'For out of the heart come evil thoughts, murder, adultery, sexual immorality, theft, false testimony, slander' (Matt. 15:10–20).

When a man or woman has no sense of inward sin, they predictably have no objectivity about themselves. They are utterly blind to their own minds, their assumptions and motives;

they become unteachable. Jesus called them 'blind' (Matt. 23:19). A person of mediocre intelligence with a sense of inward sin by the illumination of the Holy Spirit will have more objectivity about himself or herself, and will certainly be easier to live with, than a highly educated church member who can think only legalistically and see things as black or white. Blindness to our own sin takes away common sense, basic politeness and care for people's feelings. 'But the truth must be defended!' they reply. One thing you can surely say about Pharisees. They aren't very nice!

We are getting closer to the answer to the question posed above; since Pharisees were vanguards for the Law and were moral and sound on many essential matters, why didn't Jesus congratulate them? Why was he so hard on them? Even if he saw through them, that they were phoney in their righteousness, why didn't he leave them alone and attack wicked tax collectors, harlots and drunkards?

The answer is: they did so much harm. They converted people over to their party line and made that person 'twice as much a son of hell as you are' (Matt. 23:15). People like this get more excited over changing a person's theology to suit their own than they do about leading a person to Christ. They will spend more time attacking an enemy who threatens them than going into the world to save the lost. It is like King Saul who was more worried about young David than he was the archenemy of Israel – the Philistines! This is how lopsided people can get and why Jesus knew the Pharisees were dangerous. They did harm to people.

One of the hardest things Jesus said to them was this: 'You shut the kingdom of heaven in men's faces. You yourselves do not enter, nor will you let those enter who are trying to' (Matt. 23:14). This is virtually what happened to that couple I referred to before who sailed all the way from India to England in 1904 to see the Welsh Revival – but returned to India without going to Wales, because of their friends' bias against it. I have seen this happen too often. I have watched innocent people forfeit blessing that would have been theirs only because some 'mature' Christian put them off from pursuing God.

John warned, 'Watch out that you do not lose what you have worked for, but that you may be rewarded fully' (2 John 8). This verse is to be applied to one who has made great spiritual progress in their faith – well on their way to receiving a reward – but who is still vulnerable to older and 'wiser' people who might actually do them harm. There are sadly Pharisees around who spend more time lecturing to zealous new Christians and trying to change their theological views than being concerned about the world going to hell. People like this are not soul winners; they invariably fish in the Christian pond to change one's doctrinal point of view.

The hardest era Louise and I ever endured at Westminster Chapel was when we observed younger Christians being told by certain older members not to keep coming to the Chapel because the minister [me] wasn't a true man of God. This was after I brought Arthur Blessitt to preach at the Chapel. Visitors would come to hear me but would get approached by some of our older members who would say, 'There's trouble here – this is not the church for you', so a lot of these people would not come back. And yet we knew one man who was converted literally in and from the gutter and was delivered from drunkenness and poverty who eventually fell to this kind of opposition to my ministry. We knew him well. His face was aglow with his new faith. He loved me – I could feel it. We used to talk a lot. I would never have dreamed of this possibility in a thousand years, but because I did not dot the 'i's' or cross the 't's' as some legalistic people required of me, this man was warned against me and he actually turned against us. He began going to another church. That part was okay by me but I was of course disappointed. But he didn't stay long in his new church, although I never found out why. He would need new friends there, for one thing. I only know that the last thing I heard of him was that he ended up back in the world and in the gutter – and died in that state. I would justly call people Pharisees who oppose what they do not like in a church – because it does not fall within their cherished tradition – and who will 'not let those enter who are trying to'.

Therefore if you ask, 'Why would Jesus not appreciate the Pharisees but single them out as enemies – when they would seem to be on the right side of the issue?', the answer again is: they did so much harm. Then and now. Jesus knew they needed to be warned against. On one occasion he put them alongside Herod. 'Be careful', Jesus warned them. 'Watch out for the yeast of the Pharisees and that of Herod' (Mark 8:15). The disciples didn't twig at first but it eventually sunk in, 'that he was not telling them to guard against the yeast used in bread, but against the teaching of the Pharisees' (Matt. 16:12). It therefore wasn't personal; they were to guard against the teaching of these people. People are people. But if they imbibe unhealthy teaching they turn into monsters.

But Jesus also knew that Pharisees would be the ones who would lead the way to his own death. There was never a thought that such a conspiracy would be instigated by the notorious sinners of the day – drunkards, whoremongers, adulterers or even murderers. Not that they were incapable of such. But, generally speaking, people like that don't tend to send an innocent man to the cross. But religious people do. Jesus therefore had their number and declared war on them from almost the first time he opened his mouth. 'Do not think that I have come to abolish the Law', he said early on in the Sermon on the Mount (Matt. 5:17). Why say that? Why bring that subject up? It was because Jesus wanted to get to the heart of the matter as soon as possible. When he began to attack their interpretations of the Law he knew he would be in a constant battle with them from then on. It worked. They led the way in getting him crucified. But that is what he came to do! He came to die on the cross for our sins and, in the meantime, establish the kind of people who would be saved. 'I have not come to call the righteous [by which he meant those who purport to be righteous] but sinners to repentance' (Luke 5:32).

Outside Their Comfort Zone

What threatened them

The main thing that threatened Pharisees was any success enjoyed by those who did not uphold their party line. Keep in mind that the Pharisees were a party within Judaism. They wanted prestige and glory for their own party and party line. They feared being outnumbered and were therefore threatened by the common people taking so fondly to Jesus. Some thought that Jesus really was the promised Messiah. This really upset Pharisees. Therefore if Jesus enjoyed any measure of undoubted success (not that Jesus was trying to be 'successful' as such) – whether by growing crowds or performing a miracle – the Pharisees were then thrust right out of their comfort zones.

It was basically a matter of jealousy, of course. Jealousy – the sin we never see in ourselves but readily see when others have it – always intensifies when someone is pushed suddenly and without warning outside their comfort zone. When someone chooses to go outside their comfort zone because of obedience to the Lord, it is a different matter; jealousy has greater difficulty growing. But when we are threatened by another's anointing, as Saul was threatened by David (1 Sam. 18:12), our insecurity grows. Fear spreads from the crown of our heads to the soles of our feet. This is what was happening to Pharisees every time Jesus opened his mouth or performed another miracle.

Even Pontius Pilate knew that, 'knowing it was out of envy that the chief priests had handed Jesus over to them' (Mark 15:10). They were threatened by the miracles, they were threatened by Jesus' treatment of the Law and his doctrine of sin and were of course threatened by not achieving significance from the applause of people. But what really got their goat was having to watch someone outside their own party winning the hearts of the people.

'The common people heard him gladly' (Mark 12:37, AV). On one occasion they sent a temple guard to bring Jesus in so they could arrest him. But these guards came back shortly – but without Jesus. 'Why didn't you bring him in?' they were asked.

The guards replied, 'No one ever spoke the way this man does.'

'You mean he has deceived you also?' the Pharisees retorted.

This sort of thing thrust Pharisees right out of their comfort zone. They resorted to their theology: 'this mob [people following Jesus] . . . knows nothing of the law' (John 7:45–49). Their ultimate weapon against common Jews was the threat of putting anybody out of the synagogue who confessed faith in Jesus (John 12:42). The typical ploy of a Pharisee is to motivate by fear.

Their attack lay in the idea of 'guilt by association'. This tactic was used by Pharisees then and continues to be used today. If people who are attracted to you – or people you spend time with – are unworthy, theologically inarticulate, not of good stock or of respectable credentials, all of you are in the same boat together and should be regarded as being cut out of the same cloth. You are all equally guilty. You prove your guilt by those you are friendly with.

The Pharisees' trump card therefore: the kind of people that Jesus allowed to be around him, the quality of people affirming him and the backgrounds of those who were brought closest to him. 'This man welcomes sinners, and eats with them' (Luke 15:2). This, to the Pharisees, should be enough to indict Jesus as one to be shunned and should surely cause everybody to turn against Jesus! But it didn't work. Jesus even pleaded guilty to the charge and told several more parables (Luke 15 and 16) to show that the Father loves and welcomes sinners into his family.

Pharisees yesterday and today love to repudiate a person by the quality of the people they seek to reach or who admire them. Jesus surprised everybody by choosing a tax collector to be one of the twelve disciples. That was just not on! The Pharisees on the other hand quickly write off those who mix with those who do not adhere to their party line.

I received a letter from a man who ended it, 'May God have mercy on your soul' (I doubt he really wanted God to show me mercy) because I spent time with Yasser Arafat, trying to lead him to Christ. I was charged with 'guilt by association'. But I knew that Jesus would go into Ramallah. One of the closest friends I ever had broke with me because I accepted a preaching invitation he did not approve of. His reason was that it did not make him look good – since I was known to be close to him – for me to be seen preaching to that particular group of Christians. It was 'guilt by association'.

I had a close ministerial friend who refused to go into a bar to witness for Jesus. 'Why?' I asked.

'Because someone might see me go in and think I was there to have a drink', he said.

I said to him, 'Surely your life is such that people would never question why you would be there. Jesus would not care what people thought but would be right in the middle of that bar talking to sinners.'

He eventually took my advice and has since thanked me. He began to see God work in his ministry when he did not worry about his reputation. Reputation meant everything to a Pharisee who looked over his shoulder all the time to see who was watching. They wanted to preserve the Law, their 'fence' around the Law and the reputation of their forefathers who they thought were the last ones to see God work powerfully in Israel.

The Pharisees were at home when praising the great men of God of the past but threatened by the thought that God was doing something now. That God would be at work today put them right outside their comfort zones. For all of us today it is great indeed to hear of wonderful revivals of the past, of men of God who did marvellous and courageous things 200 years ago – or perhaps fifty years ago. But not today. We are in our comfort zones talking about what God did yesterday. But talk of God doing something today – unless it is in some remote island in the Third World – is too threatening to talk about. Anyone who says that what is happening now is of God will be treated with disbelief.

This was part of the offence when Jesus, having stood and read from Isaiah 61:1–2, sat down and declared, '*Today* this scripture is fulfilled in your hearing' (Luke 4:18–21). It was of great offence when Peter, speaking on the day of Pentecost, said that what was going on before their very eyes was the fulfilment of the prophet Joel's words (Acts 2:16ff.). Any reckoning that God is at work *now* makes us all uneasy; the phariseeism that lies beneath the surface breaks out in fear and suspicion.

Pharisees are even threatened by those who actually do not pose a real threat to them at all. For example, children. The ire of self-righteousness will rise in the Pharisee when children lose their heads and get involved in worshipping Jesus. This happened on Palm Sunday. 'But when the chief priests and teachers of the law saw the wonderful things he did and the children shouting in the temple area, "Hosanna to the Son of David," they were indignant' (Matt. 21:15). What do children know? How much theological training could they have received? What is more, these children were 'shouting'! That sort of thing always makes religious people uneasy! When we see kids – any young person – getting carried away under the inspiration of worship and praise, we get very uncomfortable.

We are afraid things will get out of hand! I have watched God move powerfully over the years when the children get involved. I have often thought that the next move of God on earth will witness children and young people doing mighty things for the Lord – possibly even leading the way.

How they reacted

When a Pharisee is outside his comfort zone he has to do something. One of the main things: he accuses and says, 'This is not of God.' Sometimes he crosses over a line and says, 'This is of the devil.' This is a dangerous thing to do. When this was done in the presence of Jesus and the very miraculous, he introduced a very scary teaching – the sin for which there is no forgiveness. He called it 'the blasphemy against the Holy Spirit', which makes a person guilty of an 'eternal sin' – all because they were saying of Jesus, 'He has an evil spirit' (Mark 3:28–30).

Why is it that some of us are more willing to accept that it is the devil at work than we are that something or someone is actually of God? If we have a party line that says, 'God doesn't do the miraculous nowadays – that ended after the closing of the canon of Scripture', we are forced to explain what is happening. To be on the safe side we may say a miracle takes place by a psychological reaction (this is what some said when Louise in her weakest and darkest hour was prayed for by Rodney Howard-Browne – and was instantaneously healed). But I know of some who accused Rodney of preaching in a tongue that was demonic and out of the dark regions of Africa. Whoever said it first, I don't know; I only know I would not want to be in their shoes. It is one thing to be outside your comfort zone because of reports of the miraculous – which you don't understand; it is crossing a deadline to say it is of Satan. Whatever you say, don't say that.

It is sad but sobering to realise how far we will go to defend our party line. We get defensive. Say crazy things. Get very suspicious. Send out spies, like those Jews who were sent from Jerusalem to investigate John the Baptist (John 1:19). Anyone who puts us outside our comfort zone – such as like a man whose clothes were made of camel's hair with a leather belt around his waist, calling for repentance – becomes our next target. Before it is all over we even turn on the man who was actually healed! That's what happened to the lad who was healed of blindness. Whereas he ought to have had a chance to enjoy his sight for a while he was having to explain himself and was eventually persecuted – just because he was the one who got healed (John 9:26–34)!

Those Pharisees who are thrust outside their comfort zones seem to live for the moment when they can trap the one who threatens them, catch them in an unguarded comment or find something that enables them to say 'Gotcha!' What a way to live: using your time and energy to hope someone will make a comment by which they can be labelled heretic or, at least, be embarrassed. Pharisees yesterday and today live for this. 'Then the Pharisees went out and laid hands to trap him in his words' (Matt. 22:15). When they found the woman in the act of adultery they used her 'as a trap, in order to have a basis for accusing him' (John 8:6). The moment they hope for: when they can make another lose face and be caught. People like this are not happy with themselves but will continue on and on unless God mercifully reaches down and touches their hearts –

as in the case of Nicodemus or Saul of Tarsus. That means there is the hope for all of us who are plagued by a pharisaical weakness.

The worst thing of all, however, was this. The Pharisees' search for significance outside God and from the praise of people lay at the bottom of their inability to recognise God's Messiah when he stood before their very eyes. Have you wondered why ancient Israel missed out when Messiah came? Have you wondered why they still reject him? I can tell you. It is because they chose the immediate gratification of receiving praise from people rather than to seek what it would have been like had they sought the honour that comes only from God. Seeking the honour, praise and glory that comes from God alone means letting go of the applause of men and women. It also means a lot of patience. Because you don't feel anything the first day when you make this a life-long pursuit. So it isn't easy. The Pharisees said that not only is it too hard but also they simply weren't going to go that route. Surely their reverence for the Law was good enough. The Law is God's product; the Law isn't God himself. And those who give priority to the Law inevitably end up as Pharisees and miss out on God's next move, just as the Jews missed out on their own Messiah.

Therefore Jesus was not surprised at their refusal to believe in him. He gave the explanation himself and summed up their unbelief in a simple question he asked, 'How can you [how could you possibly] believe if you accept praise from one another, yet make no effort to obtain the praise that comes from the only God?' (John 5:44). They made a choice: they preferred compliments, adoration, admiration and glory from people. Jesus said they 'made no effort' to see what it would have been like had they sought their significance in the sheer glory of God. But they opted for the glory of man. This felt better. Possibly, for a while. But at the end of the day one who makes this choice will pay for it dearly and suffer for it bitterly – forever – unless God mercifully steps down as he did in the cases of Nicodemus and Saul of Tarsus. And me. And I hope you.

What breaks your heart is that the Pharisees were the ones who led to Jesus' weeping over the city of Jerusalem, in a lengthy denunciation of the Pharisees in Matthew 23. It culminated in Jesus crying out,

O Jerusalem, Jerusalem, you who kill the prophets and stone those sent to you, how often I have longed to gather your children together, as a hen gathers her chicks under her wings, but you were not willing. Look, your house is left to you desolate. (Matt. 22:37–38)

8

Twenty-six Reasons
You May Be a Pharisee

'It is a test of a good religion whether you can joke about it'
G.K. Chesterton

A few years ago someone sent me a humorous booklet of
cartoons entitled 'You are a Redneck if . . .' by Jeff Foxworthy.
I have racked my brain to see if there is a British equivalent of
an American 'redneck'. Unless you have travelled the United
States or watched a lot of American television you would have
difficulty in grasping what we mean by 'rednecks'. He is
someone who never lies in the sun to get a tan but is always
fiery red on the back of his neck because he wears a tee shirt
and works in the sun. He is associated with ignorance and
virtually no culture. The booklet is written to get people to
see that they themselves might just be a redneck if certain

things apply to them, such as: you take a load to the dump [rubbish tip] and bring back more than you took; you had to remove your toothpick from your wedding pictures; your dad walks you to school because you're both in the same year; you think Sherlock Holmes is a housing project in Mississippi.

My colleague Jack Taylor used a phrase in a sermon, 'Chances are you are a Pharisee if ...' and I have been intrigued by the idea ever since. We all need to learn to laugh at ourselves and not be defensive when our weakness is touched on. Meekness, a great virtue, could be defined as the ability to accept a hard criticism without being the slightest bit defensive. A certain measure of meekness is required to work through this chapter because I think it hits all of us. I lead the way, I assure you, in being an expert in phariseeism because too much that follows continues to hit me between the eyes. I am not proud of this. But I want you to know I do not see myself as being fully emancipated from this bondage. And yet we are going to look further at the very sins that angered our Lord Jesus most.

Sometimes we ourselves get angry at church, even in a prayer meeting. Prayer meetings are the backbone of a good church but can also be the most painfully boring times of the week. This is because there are those who love to hear themselves pray – and drive others mad. My friend Harry Kilbride, who lives not far from us in Florida, told me of two incidents in one of his former churches in which people had to be lovingly rebuked for their long prayers. In one case, a man would pray week after week – the same prayer that went on and on before getting to the petitions: 'We praise thee, O God, for thy love, thy sovereignty, thy omnipotence, this wonderful salvation you have given in sending thy Son . . .' On and on the man would go.

Harry knew this man kept others from praying and was in danger of making people run away, especially young people whom he wanted to encourage to come. So he made a public appeal to those who came that 'perhaps not everybody would pray every single week'. The man never came back to the prayer meeting again. It seems he did not care to be truly involved in prayer, only as long as he could pray his long prayers.

The second incident had to do with a lady who prayed much the same way. In this case Dr Kilbride asked her to see him in the vestry. He asked if she enjoyed the prayer meetings and how she thought they were going. 'Oh wonderful, pastor', she said. He then, as gently as he could – sugar-coating the medicine – asked her if perhaps she might pray not every single week but perhaps once every three weeks in order to encourage others, especially young people, to pray. The woman agreed. The problem was, after then, she only came once every three weeks – and she would then pray! She too was not interested in coming unless she prayed.

These are examples of how Pharisees, though good people in so many ways, are alive and well in the Church today. In Westminster Chapel we had a sweet old lady (now in heaven) who prayed aloud every time there was a prayer meeting and would not finish a prayer without condemning those who weren't present. 'Lord, you know there are so few of us here. So many don't care to come to a prayer meeting. So many don't love you. They don't want to carry the load. They don't want to intercede . . .' On and on she would go. It had the effect of making all present sigh the moment she began, and we wished she could somehow manage to pray without pointing the finger! It is a subtle form of phariseeism. It is a religious spirit, one of the hardest nuts to crack in the Church today. It is the enemy of what God wants to do in the here and now.

If, however, phariseeism makes us angry when we see it in others, we need to see it in ourselves and how it must equally grieve the Holy Spirit! Jesus's words perfectly mirrored what the Father wanted said (John 5:19), and we can be equally sure that the Holy Spirit, who is the Spirit of Christ, feels the same things Jesus felt. And yet it is easy to see it in others; can we see this in ourselves?

This is why this chapter is important. If certain aspects of the Pharisees raised the holy ire of the Son of God – who was devoid of self-righteousness – I want to be sure I am convicted of phariseeism in my own heart and life and am doing everything I possibly can to be unlike the ancient Pharisees of Jesus' day.

What is the possibility that you and I could be a Pharisee? What are the signs – or warning signals? Chances are you and I are Pharisees if . . .

1 We love to point the finger

It comes easily. And the devil does it best. He is called 'the accuser' (Rev. 12:10). You must choose whether you want to play the devil and point the finger or be Jesus who lets us save face. Jesus actually gave us a selfish motivation for not pointing the finger. 'Do not judge, and you will not be judged' (Luke 6:37). I will forfeit the benefit of this promise if I play the role of accuser. On the other hand, if I choose the pointing of the finger rather than let God sort out the person I want to condemn, I too 'will be judged' (Matt. 7:1). Believe me, I know this to be true by experience! It is safe and far better to cease pointing the finger – ever again. You will never be sorry.

2 We love to say 'Gotcha'

We love to catch the person in the act whereby they cannot deny they got caught. Or to get to see them squirm when they are found out. It is said that a journalist's dream is to write an article or book in order to say 'Gotcha' – like finding someone highly respected, such as Billy Graham or Mother Teresa, and exposing their imperfections. God knows we all have skeletons in the cupboard and if he decided to tell the world what he knows about us we would die on the spot. But there is a better way to live. Joseph fantasised that he would see the dream fulfilled of his brothers bowing down to him – after the wicked thing they did to him – and say 'Gotcha' to them. But when the dream was actually fulfilled he was a changed man and, instead of looking at them with glee in their helpless state, he wept over them and totally forgave them (Gen. 45:1–11). That was the secret of his greatness and the reason God trusted him with such a lofty status.

3 We are good at sending people on a 'guilt trip'

The Law invariably finds people guilty. When you have interpretations of the Law that exceed the Law – or rules of your own that you think are valid – it only widens the scope for the possibility of guilt. And when we superimpose our rules and wishes on friends or enemies in order to require that they come up to our standard we become Pharisees. They loved to make people feel guilty. God is not that way. Believe it or not, once we are justified by faith in Christ alone and walking by faith, God does not want any of us to feel guilty. On the contrary, he gives us the Holy Spirit whereby we say to him, 'Abba, Father' (Rom. 8:15). When the guilt is gone and we have fellowship with the Father, the joy is greater than any this world can offer. Total forgiveness means we do not send another person on a guilt trip; we are aware of what we have been forgiven and we treat others as God has treated us.

4 We require standards of people that are not written in Scripture

I grew up in a church in which they often spoke of 'standards'. Godly standards. I could not go to movies as a child. My mother did not wear lipstick. My father would not take a Sunday newspaper. I could not play ball on Sunday. Some preachers in my old denomination seemed to try to outdo each other on how strict you could be. I always felt sorry for the teenage girls in my church because they were the only ones in their school who could not wear make-up. When we impose rules on people – even though we might justify them for some reason or another – that are not solidly written in the Word of God we risk being the Pharisees of our day. It only adds to people's bondage. I urged members of Westminster Chapel to pray thirty minutes a day but it was never a requirement. It was not a rule, only a suggestion. But standards are rules that people must live by – or be 'out' rather than 'in'. God does not like this. Pharisees do.

5 We practise 'guilt by association'

We accuse people of being unclean, unrighteous or out of order when they mix with people of other faiths, of varying views or questionable lifestyles. If I accept an invitation to preach to a group with whom I do not agree theologically, does it make me guilty of condoning what they believe? No. But some would accuse me. Pharisees would. Not Jesus. If I invite a person to preach for me but who happens to hold to views I am uncomfortable with, does this make me guilty by having this person in my pulpit? No. If I pray with a fellow Christian who is not totally at one with me doctrinally does that make me guilty by associating with them in this way? No. But if I accuse you of being a 'sinner' because you are having a meal with a 'sinner' then I am a Pharisee. If I try to make you feel shameful because of who you choose to spend time with, I am a Pharisee.

6 We assume something or someone is of the devil when someone's ministry makes us uncomfortable

The Pharisees could not deny that Jesus performed miracles. If they said that these miracles were done by God it would have condoned Jesus' behaviour and put them to shame. So they resorted to a trick that has been repeated many times since: they attributed what was done to the devil. In this even Martin

Luther became a Pharisee. He actually once said of his rival, Ulrich Zwingli (1484–1531), 'Zwingli's God is my devil' because of differing views regarding the Lord's Supper. If you and I are threatened by someone's success and notice how popular they are but have no answer but to say 'They are of the devil', we are Pharisees. It is fair to say they are misguided or in theological error. But to claim they are of the devil is dangerous stuff. If you or I ever say this we had better be right. The Pharisees had no hesitation and so do modern Pharisees who resort to the ultimate put-down in order to make their opponents look bad. Jesus would not do that.

7 We say that a person is 'not a Christian' if they disagree with us

That is judging just like the Pharisees did. It is the quick cop-out, it is our way of punishing the person we disagree with. Instead of saying politely that they for some reason disagree with us we glibly say, 'These people aren't even saved.' There is always the possibility in some cases of course that those who attack us are not truly converted. But why say that? Why not give them the benefit of the doubt? Why resort to the ultimate insult just because they don't agree with us? It is almost childish to label a person an unbeliever just because they don't agree with us. Even if they are unsaved, if we treat them with love and dignity, they may be converted one day and will love and respect us for the way we treated them in the meantime. A good rule of thumb: when you fall out with a person, treat them with such dignity that they will respect you when you make up! Pharisees don't want to make up with people.

8 We esteem 'the way we've always done it' above change even when the latter is not heretical

Remember that the Pharisees made the Word of God of no effect by their traditions (Matt. 15:6). Their own traditions were based not on Scripture but their peculiar rules. When new ways emerge but which are not contrary to Scripture, beware of falling into the trap of always wanting the 'old wine'. Those who say, 'The old is better' (Luke 5:39) want to stay in their comfort zones – to keep the taste they are used to. All new movements God raises up require change. Every person described in Hebrews 11 had to move out of their comfort zones. They broke with tradition. At Westminster Chapel I had a fight on my hands because I wanted the organist to play 'Turn your eyes upon Jesus' as a prelude rather than Mozart. The latter, I was told – not by the organist – made our Willis pipe organ sound better. My old friend and assistant Jon Bush used to say that the last seven words of a dying church were: 'We never did it that way before.'

9 We do not practise what we preach

Jesus plainly said of Pharisees that they 'do not practise what they preach' (Matt. 23:3). I cannot think of a greater hypocrisy on the planet than demanding of another person what I would not do myself. What turned Gandhi against Christianity was Christians. The greatest testimony we could give to the world is not our articulate theology or eloquent way of presenting it but their discovery that we are real – that we really do practise what we preach. This does not mean we are perfect or never sin. 'If we claim to be without sin, we deceive ourselves and the truth is not in us' (1 John 1:8). But if our faces, hearts and lives reflect the love of Jesus, people are going to want what we've got. As a Muslim businessman said to Arthur Blessitt in a bar in Jordan, 'I want what you've got' – referring to Arthur's countenance.

'Twas not the truth you taught, to you so clear, to me so
  dim;
But when you came to me you brought a sense of Him.
Yes from your eyes He beckoned me, and from your heart
His love was shed,
And I lost sight of you and saw the Christ instead.

Anon

10 We are more comfortable talking about the mighty movements of God yesterday than today

It will be recalled that the Pharisees thought themselves pious and faithful because they decorated the tombs of the prophets. The Pharisees even fancied that they would have recognised God at work and would not have been critical of what God was doing had they been around in previous generations. It is like saying we would not have crucified Jesus had we been around at that time. This is sheer self-righteousness. We all crucified Jesus. We all are critical of what God is up to in the here and now – it always means going outside our comfort zone – unless he opens our eyes. It is also wrong to dismiss what is happening today because it does not repeat exactly what was happening before. There was no clear precedent that

I know of for what characterised the Welsh Revival. God does not always do the same thing twice in any case. We must be willing to lose face for God's glory and recognise that God may be working right before our eyes. The offence is to say this *is* God at work now.

11 We take ourselves too seriously

The Pharisees thought they were God's 'remnant' and it was up to them to preserve the Law by their traditions. They took themselves very seriously by the attention they demanded, the way they dressed, the way they tried to trap Jesus, demanding to be called 'Rabbi', insisting on seats of honour. This is the lifestyle of a Pharisee and it is not a good sign at all when we take ourselves very seriously. This means we can't laugh at ourselves – certainly we can't cope with being laughed at, listen to criticism without being defensive or be passed by without sulking when we thought we should be invited. The most secure people are those who can laugh at themselves, accept criticism without being defensive or be passed over when they thought they should have been consulted or invited. The main psychological problem of the Pharisees was that they were insecure.

12 We judge by outward appearance

This borders on 'guilt by association' but is slightly different. I refer to when we don't like the way a person dresses – too fashionable, too expensive or too casual; we don't like their accent – too posh or too working-class; we don't approve of their education or lack of it – or where they received it; we don't approve of their theological or church background; we judge them by their neighbourhood; we don't approve of their employment; we don't like their friends. Pharisees are past masters at this. People criticised Arthur Blessitt because he wore jeans in our pulpit. I was criticised when I stopped wearing a Geneva gown. These are things that should not come into our minds. Unless we want to be the Pharisees of our day.

13 We are preoccupied by our appearance

It will be recalled that Pharisees strutted around in their garb because 'Everything they do is done for men to see', said Jesus (Matt. 23:5). This does not mean we are oblivious to the way we are seen in public. Of course not. I want to look nice. I make sure my hair is combed and that I have had a clean shave. But if I seek significance by my appearance, my clothes or whether or not I wear a suit or tie, I have lapsed into a pharisaical mode that is certainly not good.

14 We care more about people's opinions than God's

When Jesus said that the Jews could not believe in his Messiahship because they preferred the 'praise' of one another (rather than making an effort to receive God's praise) the Greek word in John 5:44 is *doxa* which means glory, honour or praise. It comes from a root word that means 'opinion'. This means that God has an opinion. We must make a choice: whose opinion matters? If we care more about what people think, we are Pharisees. What is gravely serious about this is the very point I have made: by making 'no effort to obtain' God's praise, or opinion, they set themselves up for unbelief. Thus when the very Messiah they claimed they longed for came and was right under their noses, they did not recognise him. All because they developed a habit of wanting the praise of people rather than of God. This may seem a fairly innocuous tendency – since it is surely human to want people to compliment us – but making no effort to obtain his compliment of them ended up cutting off their hope of seeing and enjoying God work in their own day. Speaking personally, of all the points I am listing in this part of the book, this one is the premiss I value most of all. I fear more than anything else in the world that I should want your approval of me more than God's.

15 We need to be sure people know about it if we give, pray or fast

You will recall that Jesus told us not to be like those who only gave, prayed or fasted when it would be seen by other people. Why was this so important? It is important because the principle just looked at above – that of John 5:44 – is at stake. Jesus made it clear: if we do what we do to be seen of men we get our reward; yes, but it is only in the here and now – the feeling that builds up our egos: the praise of people not of God. The irony is, we develop the healthiest egos, significance and sense of self-esteem when we cultivate a habit of seeking only the praise of God. God has a way of doubling our sense of significance and self-esteem. He will not let us down. But when we choose to give, pray or fast only when people are likely to find out, we risk repeating the fatal sin of the ancient Jews who utterly missed out on what God wanted them to receive. The same missing out can happen today as well.

16 We are motivated by money

You will recall that the Pharisees 'loved money' and were motivated by the love of money. It was an important insight by Luke (Luke 16:14). It should not be surprising. For when all else is said about Pharisees it follows that a love of money would be very close by. What will make it easy for us to turn loose our money is the promise of people finding out that we gave! This shows that pride runs almost parallel with our love of money. In other words, we hang on to our cash and assets, but if someone dangles a promise that our giving, whether to a church or charity, will be known by our getting special recognition and credit, the motivation to give is increased adequately to make us give. God gets no glory in this case, neither do we receive a reward from him; only the 'reward' that people say, 'How good of you to do that.' What is more telling, however, is that we spend lavishly on ourselves and feel totally at ease. What we buy adds to our prestige and causes others to feel envious – which we love to think is happening with them.

17 We feel righteous by comparing ourselves to others

Rather than measuring ourselves by the Word of God we measure others. Instead of discovering the sinfulness of our own hearts, which is so painful, we immediately find someone nearby who we judge to be in bad shape and assume, by contrast, we are okay. But that is by comparison. Besides, we don't know what is in another's heart. Therefore when we get a righteous feeling by selecting somebody we assume to be more wicked than ourselves, we totally avoid the very things Jesus wants us to do; namely, to see what we are like before God and not in the eyes of people. The tax collector was justified because he felt so unworthy before God (Luke 18:13–14); the Pharisee was not justified because the only way he could feel good was to compare himself to the sinful tax collector. He felt better about himself but had no idea how he appeared before God. This is the very reason a Pharisee lacks objectivity about himself and is so superficial: he gets his smug feeling by finding someone he can look down on – and never gives the matter another thought.

18 We have no sense of sin by our thoughts – only our deeds

The Pharisees were 'offended' by the teaching that what makes a person unclean is 'what come out of his mouth' rather than what goes in (Matt. 15:11–12). A good rule of thumb in assessing whether we are Pharisees is how we get a sense of sin. If it is only in what we do then we can get off the hook quite a bit. The Pharisees could only conceive of sin in terms of outward acts – as in most of the Ten Commandments. They never dwell on the Tenth Commandment, which has to do with the heart; namely coveting, which is what convinced the righteous Saul of Tarsus that he really was a sinner after all (Rom. 7:7–9). My own theological background did not prepare me for this most powerful and essential insight – that sin is in our thoughts as well as our deeds. What ultimately convinced me, apart from the conviction through the immediate and direct witness of the Spirit, was John's words, 'If we claim to be without sin, we deceive ourselves and the truth is not in us' (1 John 1:8). Therefore if we claim to be without sin, merely because we haven't done anything such as being sexually immoral, we are first self-deceived and second devoid of the truth.

19 We major on minors

We do this in a thousand ways of course, but the example Jesus gave when he said that Pharisees 'strain out a gnat but swallow a camel' had to do with tithing (Matt. 23:23–24). A Pharisee is one who avoids personal obligation to the whole Law by keeping some of it; namely, rules which give them a good feeling that they are okay. Tithing does this nicely. If someone tithes, they tell themselves, 'I must be okay' because 'Most people don't'. Moreover, they make sure they tithe by doing it across the board – tithing spices such as mint, dill and cumin. Nothing is left out. Never mind that there are weightier matters of the Law – like justice (caring for the poor), mercy (showing kindness to strangers) and faithfulness twenty-four hours a day to the entire world; if we prove that we tithe, this counts for righteousness somehow (we tell ourselves). I found it was sometimes easier to get Christians to tithe at Westminster Chapel than it was to get them out on the streets witnessing on a Saturday morning – or totally to forgive their enemies. It is like the rules in Jerusalem today. There are those who excuse all manner of sins but they make sure they uphold dietary laws, such as 'Do not cook a young goat in its mother's milk' (Exod. 23:19), which (when brought forward to today) means do not put mayonnaise on a beef sandwich.

20 We are experts in finding loopholes in the Law to excuse certain areas of disobedience

One of the rules of the ancient Pharisees – which was not part of the Law but part of their 'fence' around the Law – was a way of avoiding responsibility to parents. Whereas the Law states, 'Honour your father and mother' the Pharisees said that 'Whatever help you [the parents] might otherwise have received from me [your son] is a gift devoted to God', that he is not to 'honour his father' with it. Money that should have been given to parents was diverted to the synagogue or temple. This way the Pharisee could divert money that was to be earmarked for his parents to the synagogue. Thus Jesus said, 'You break the command of God for the sake of your tradition' (Matt. 15:3–6). The Pharisee reasoned, 'My parents don't need the money but the synagogue does.' We can do that today in many ways. For example, my church (the storehouse) doesn't need the money; I need to pay my bills which God would want me to do. We create our own loopholes. For example, we excuse ourselves from forgiving another because 'They are not sorry', 'They have not apologised', 'I don't have to forgive them unless they repent first'. Our model is to be Jesus, not the Pharisees. Nobody repented at the sight of the crucifixion and yet he said, 'Father, forgive them, for they do not know what they are doing' (Luke 23:34).

21 We are more concerned to uphold our theology than to help people

We saw how the Pharisees could not bring themselves to rejoice that a blind man was healed because the healing took place on the Sabbath. It is good when we hold sound theology high in our priorities. I am a theologian and I love theology. But there comes a time that I must accept that God will use a person who is not in agreement with my thinking. When God uses a person whose theology I could pick to pieces, which is more important – to scold him for his error, or rejoice that God uses such a person to see people blessed, healed and delivered? Not to rejoice in someone being blessed, no matter the instrument God chooses, merely because I don't agree with the person, makes me a Pharisee. God may use one whose theology is different, whose church is different and whose culture is different. I should affirm what God does through a person I may not particularly like.

22 We love to score theological points with our enemies

Two of the ancient parties in Judaism were the Pharisees (in some ways the fundamentalists of their day) and the Sadducees (in some ways the liberals of their day). They had in common a hatred for Jesus but each still got their thrills from making their rivals look bad. When the Pharisees noted gleefully that Jesus had 'silenced' the Sadducees with his argument against them regarding resurrection (Matt. 22:34), they immediately wanted to have their turn at challenging Jesus. In other words, while opposing Jesus both Pharisees and Sadducees took shots at each other; this sort of thing got them worked up and excited. The apostle Paul knew this and played into the rivalry brilliantly when he was being tried. He said before the Sanhedrin that he was on trial because of his hope in the resurrection of the dead. 'When he said this, a dispute broke out between the Pharisees and the Sadducees, and the assembly was divided.' The episode got Paul out of a difficult situation and bought him more time (Acts 23:6–10)! I am reminded of two churches in Alabama, one a Methodist (who believed you could lose your salvation if you sinned) the other a Baptist (who believed once saved, always saved). The two churches ran missions concurrently but the Baptists were heard to say later, 'Well; we didn't have much of a revival, but thank God the Methodists didn't either.' Vintage phariseeism.

23 We claim God's approval of us rather than our rivals because we know our theology, not theirs, is sound

The party spirit that emerged from the rivalry between Sadducees and Pharisees kept them apart and fuelled their motivation to score points. But at bottom the Pharisees knew that God must be with them rather than their opponents because of such teachings as the resurrected life beyond the grave and belief in angels. The Sadducees did not believe in these and the Pharisees knew absolutely these truths were solidly based in their Law and traditions; therefore God would decidedly be on their side. This gave them a superior feeling. They did not merely think – they knew – they were on the side of the angels. It did not seem to bother them at all that right before their eyes was God's very Son who they did not recognise. It is so easy for us to take ourselves so seriously because we know God would be on the side of the party who is sounder! Really? He may well feel toward us as Jesus did the Pharisees.

24 We easily dismiss a person we don't want to like because we are able to find something truly wrong with them

This is an old pharisaical tactic – find something you know is really wrong; therefore you are at utter peace in rejecting that person entirely. The Pharisees found what they were looking for: Jesus claimed to be able to forgive sins. What? Forgive sins? Blasphemy! Who can forgive sins but God alone? Jesus calmly asked, 'Which is easier: to say, "Your sins are forgiven," or to say, "Get up and walk"?' (Luke 5:21–23). We do this too. When we hope we don't have to accept someone we look for something we know is absolutely wrong in them; therefore we have the excuse we needed not to affirm them. 'He doesn't believe in the Rapture.' 'This man doesn't believe in the millennium.' 'This person speaks in tongues.' 'This person has not been baptised in the Holy Spirit.' When we find what we are looking for we tell ourselves, 'Don't worry about affirming this person – you know what is seriously wrong in them.' I knew of one preacher who rejected Dr James Kennedy's method of winning souls (called Evangelism Explosion) because Dr Kennedy does not believe in a literal one-thousand-year reign of Jesus on the earth after the Second Coming.

25 We say, 'We are more in tune with God than you are'

This works several ways, but let me mention two of them. First, take people known as being 'charismatic'. So many of them, I fear (they certainly give the impression), honestly think they are more spiritual than others. 'If you don't speak in tongues, you are not as spiritual as I am.' Or, 'If you haven't experienced the gifts of the Spirit, you are not really in touch with God.' Such people make some Evangelical Christians feel second-class and this attitude, which I can only call pharisaical, helps erect a wall that divides Christians from Christians. But second, take the Calvinists. So many of them, I fear (they certainly give the impression), honestly think they are more on God's wavelength than other Christians. 'If you don't believe in the sovereignty of God as we do, you are not a faithful believer.' Or, 'If you don't believe in predestination and the eternal security of the believer, you don't really know the God of the Bible.' Such a spirit, which I can only call pharisaical, alienates many other Christians and makes some of them feel they are theologically illiterate. As you can see, there is more than one kind of Pharisee!

26 We call another person a Pharisee

If I call you a Pharisee, I am a Pharisee. When I say, 'The trouble with you is that you are always judging people', I just then judged you. When I point the finger at you for pointing the finger, I too point the finger. 'Do not judge, or you too will be judged' (Matt. 7:1). What does one do? Answer: we must learn to control the tongue. 'God is in heaven and you are on earth, so let your words be few' (Eccles. 5:2). 'When words are many, sin is not absent, but he who holds his tongue is wise' (Prov. 10:19).

The truth is, the Pharisee lurks in all of us. This means we would be among those Jesus condemned the most. This fact alone ought to catapult us out of our comfort zones and make us see not only our self-righteousness but also how grateful we should be that God saved us. We don't deserve to be saved. God was simply kind. Good. Merciful. He saved Saul of Tarsus, a Pharisee of the Pharisees indeed. And Saul, called Paul, never got over it. He thanked God as best he could as long as he lived.

If God could save Paul, he could save anybody. If God could save you, he could save anybody. If God could save me, he could save anybody. Why did he do it? I don't know and probably will never know. I can only spend the rest of my life doing my best to thank him and show him how thankful I am.